DIVINE MOTHER HEALING

*Vibrational Healing Tools for Your Body,
Mind, and Spirit*

BY CONNIE HUEBNER
WITH SANDRA MACKENZIE

BALBOA.PRESS
A DIVISION OF HAY HOUSE

Balboa Press books may be ordered through booksellers or by contacting:

Balboa Press
A Division of Hay House
1663 Liberty Drive
Bloomington, IN 47403
www.balboapress.com
1 (877) 407-4847

Because of the dynamic nature of the Internet, any web addresses or links contained in this book may have changed since publication and may no longer be valid. The views expressed in this work are solely those of the author and do not necessarily reflect the views of the publisher, and the publisher hereby disclaims any responsibility for them.

Reverend Connie Huebner is an ordained minister and her work is spiritually based. She believes healing is based on a connection to Divine energy. Neither she nor the publisher assume any legal responsibility for the effectiveness, results, or benefits of reading this book or using the methods described. Neither Connie Huebner nor the publisher make any promises, warranties, or guarantees about the results of her healing work or the Divine Guidance that she receives and relays to people. Divine Mother Guidance and Healing sessions help many people, but like any modality, they may not work for everyone, and individual results will vary.

The author is not a medical doctor, attorney, psychiatrist, therapist, or other licensed health professional. She does not diagnose, cure, heal, or treat disease, or give psychological treatment. She recommends that people see a licensed medical professional for their medical, emotional, or mental problems. Her Divine Mother Guidance and Healing work is not a substitute for medical diagnosis or treatment.

ISBN: 978-1-9822-1639-9 (sc)
ISBN: 978-1-9822-1638-2 (e)

Print information available on the last page.

Balboa Press rev. date: 07/09/2020

Contents

Acknowledgments

Thank you to those whose work has inspired me, taught me, and given me deeper insight into healing. I want to thank Maharishi Mahesh Yogi, founder of Transcendental Meditation and the Science of Creative Intelligence, who gave me access to the ancient Vedic wisdom of life and profoundly deepened my experience of Oneness. I live in deep gratitude to him for the knowledge of consciousness.

Other teachers I wish to thank are Dr. Peter Meyer, founder/president of the Teaching of Intuitional Metaphysics, Inc., for his classes on speaking to Divine Beings; and Rich Bell, founder of Ascending Light, Limited, who inspired me to create a way to facilitate a deep healing in consciousness that transforms a person's life.

My profound gratitude goes to Sandra MacKenzie, without whom this book would not have materialized. She is a saint—with her patience, compassion, and tenacity, she kept me focused on completing this material through many ups and downs, transformations, and distractions. Her heart is immense, her kindness unfailing, her forgiveness constant. Sandy is an accomplished writer herself who helped me frame this subtle vibrational knowledge in practical heart-based language.

Deep appreciation to Don Lisefski, who had the vision and drive to use the World Wide Web to bring the Divine Mother material to an international audience. Don masterminded a new, more extensive website that was instrumental in expanding the scope of my work with Divine Mother.

I want to thank my longtime friend, author Susan Shumsky, for all her help and encouragement over the years. Susan has supported my work from its beginning by publishing my early Transformational Prayers in her own books, listing me on her website, and selling my recordings in her travels. Susan has encouraged me for many years to write a book and has been generous with her time and helpful advice as I have put this book together.

My hat goes off to Jim Shead for his meticulous work of formatting, final editing, and follow-up on all details to create this publication. Deep appreciation goes to Marci Freeman for her invaluable help with the early editing and refining of this material. And immense gratitude to Eric Randall for his creativity and persistence in designing the cover of this book.

I extend a great "thank you" to Gillian Peirce who lovingly assisted me in my work for many years. She spent hours patiently formatting this material, interfacing with the publisher, and making sure all details were completed. Gillian was a great being and loyal friend.

Helen French and Stephen Black helped me refine the wording of the Healing Tools and pushed me into the public offering of my work. Their friendship has been a deep source of nourishment from the beginning of this journey.

Thanks to Sonia Gunderson, who supported and expanded my connection to a wider audience in the early days and whose brilliant organizing power built the foundations of my organization.

Pam Harding and June Oliver have tirelessly supported my work and teachings for many years with their clarity, insights, and skills. I extend my deep appreciation for their tremendous support.

There are others who have made important contributions to my work. Rob Jollymore helped craft the Divine Truth methodology. Francesca Hoerlein and Kathryn Bell helped me write preliminary versions of this material. Colleen Bell, Coral Scranton, Mark Hanson, Susan Walch, and Elinor Hall all offered me significant assistance at the beginning of this endeavor. I have immense appreciation for each of you.

I am grateful to everyone who has ever had a private session with me or taken a class. You have all contributed to the refinement of the material in this book.

I want to acknowledge my husband David and my children Elizabeth and David for keeping me grounded, practical, and centered as I explored the unbounded depths of my inner life. You have anchored me on my path and in my heart with your unconditional love. I wish to especially recognize my husband David for committing, with me, to a lifetime of spiritual awakening.

Foreword

For quite some time, the personal relationship I have with Divine Mother has been growing very nicely. But when I started participating in Connie Huebner's Divine Mother programs around five years ago, that relationship began deepening profoundly—and with that there came many good changes to my life: more love, happiness, confidence.

Divine Mother wants a deep personal relationship with all of us. She wants us all to return to Her … to our eternal home with Her. Therefore, in our world now, the Divine is expressing very strongly as Divine Mother, for we desperately need Her nurturing, compassionate, and highly creative qualities to unify our human family. Indeed, to counter the negativity and divisiveness we are seeing, an expansion of Her sweet, loving influence is vitally needed in the world now—not only for humanity's continued progress—but for its very survival.

Yet we can have much hope in all this, for there are undercurrents, a beautiful stirring, of Divine Mother's powerful influence emerging. Yes, I know, these undercurrents do not appear so much in the daily news, yet indications are becoming increasingly evident. And one of the more powerful undercurrents is the presence of Connie Huebner and her programs. She is a clear and beautiful instrument of Divine Mother, and I regard her as at the forefront of this stirring, this movement, of Divine Mother in the world today. As Connie explains in this book, it is Divine Mother who is leading her in the development and use of these Healing Tools.

Now let's turn to the book itself. The book you now hold in your hands is fundamentally different from just about any other you will encounter. Many spiritual books describe exciting experiences, states of consciousness, etc., but usually these books only provide inspiring reading, and in that way, they do have their value. But this book differs in that it is really a how-to book—and I know from experience: it works. The Healing Tools presented here actually do heal.

The Divine Mother Healing Tools operate at the deepest levels of our being to heal both surface concerns, such as relationship and finances, and inner wounds, especially those wounds that keep us in separation—separation from each other, from Nature, from the Divine, from ourselves—even from our own very deepest level of self, the Infinite.

So now with this book, you have a very powerful set of Healing Tools, and with them you are able to work directly with the Infinite Source through an intimate connection with Divine Mother. And She is always there, deep in your heart, ready and waiting for you to accept Her invitation to realize more fully the beautiful and powerful Divine Being you are.

Fairfield, Iowa   James L. Shead
March 4, 2020   Certified Divine Mother Practitioner

Part One

My Personal Journey of Discovering the Divine Feminine

Chapter 1

The Beginning

In the fall of 1968 I had the defining moment of my life. Everything for the rest of my life has been influenced by that one moment. What happened to me wasn't obvious on the outside, but it rocked my inner world and changed the way I thought about everything. It was as if I had been given a superpower, though I never used it and didn't tell anyone about it. They would have thought I was crazy. I had found the way to find every answer, let go of every fear, and never be lost again.

Early Life

I was never particularly spiritual in my youth. God didn't interest me, church was boring, and I became an atheist at age 18. Now I am an ordained minister, have founded a church, originated a system of energy healing, and have a powerful and intimate relationship with Divine Mother. This is the story of how I got here.

As a child I was most interested in playing and exploring the countryside around our small-town Michigan home, climbing trees, and having Tom Sawyer-like adventures with my friends, never thinking about God. I was always up to some mischief. My adventures sometimes got me into trouble, but I usually surfaced with my head above the water.

When we got caught smoking cigarettes sitting on the garage roof, my friend Susie got a spanking. I got a lecture. Whew, I got off easy! We loved to ring doorbells and run away, peeking and laughing as the people came to the door. Until they called our parents!

I dreamed of having one impossible thing in my life…a black horse. I knew I couldn't get a horse of my own, so my bicycle became my black horse, and I would ride around the neighborhood imagining I was galloping across the fields. I wished for that black horse on every evening star, birthday candle, fallen eyelash, and lucky stone for years. Until unexpectedly, and for no apparent reason to me, my parents announced I could get a horse! We looked everywhere until I found him. He was shiny black and waiting for me. It didn't matter if he wasn't fully trained. It didn't matter that he bucked me off the first time I rode him. He was my black horse coming to me from all my wishes. What I thought was impossible became real, and I learned the impossible was within reach. Wishes come true.

I was in love with the stars to the point of memorizing the constellations. Fascinated with the cosmos, I would gaze at the heavens, awed and serene, locating planets, thrilled by shooting stars, captivated by the shimmering aurora borealis. The mystery of the sky drew me into its dance and expanded my mind.

I wanted to be two things when I grew up: a lion tamer and president of the United States. The lion tamer job was for excitement and thrills. The president job came from my awareness of suffering and pain in the world.

Every night at dinner my father led a discussion of world events, and I learned that my haven of comfort and security to dream my dreams and explore my world in safety was not everyone's privilege. The world was in crisis and kept getting worse. I wondered why no one was doing anything about fixing things. For some reason, I thought I knew how. It appeared that no one else did or it would have been fixed long ago, so I decided to do it. I figured I would become the first woman president of the United States. It was that simple. I would do something about it.

Puberty was a drag. I didn't want to grow up. Peter Pan was my idea of a great life. To be a child forever was my dream of perfection, so I resisted puberty by flattening my chest with tight undershirts and refusing to shave my legs.

But I couldn't stop Mother Nature and finally surrendered to adolescence, now exploring that with Tom Sawyer's capacity for adventure. I tried smoking, alcohol, sneaking out of the house at night, dating and the usual pranks and parties of high school. I liked thinking that this was living slightly on the wild side.

College Days

When college came along, I continued to develop my capacity for savoring all of life. I spent two years at Bradford Junior College, a small eastern women's college near Boston, Massachusetts, and then transferred to the University of North Carolina in Chapel Hill, a large vibrant southern university. Having already decided that life was for enjoyment, I sought to explore the variety of experience, have fun, learn what I could, and take every adventure that came along.

While in school near Boston, I went to poetry readings by Allen Ginsberg. I investigated the Richard Alpert and Timothy Leary experiments with LSD. I regularly attended smoke-filled clubs where soon-to-be famous jazz artists performed. One of my friends was dating a jazz musician, so we had an inside peek into that world. I felt that I was following the pulse of the times.

In my sophomore year, I decided to be an atheist. God didn't make sense to me. I'd thought about it for a long time. One dark night in the back of a bus, I fell into deep contemplation about my spiritual life. I was raised Episcopalian, but never connected to it. The values and principles my father lived by and the unconditional love my mother demonstrated were far more meaningful than anything I got from an unknown God in the sky. I was finished with Him. That night, I gave a farewell speech to God, stating that if He existed He would have to prove it to me, but until then I was now officially a non-believer and would not be involved in any communication attempts, church attendance, or participation in His, obvious to me, false legacy on earth. God and I parted ways.

The last two years in Chapel Hill became a whirlwind of dating, fraternity parties, and rock concerts. After the all-women's college, I was ready to party, and I went out every single night! Recreational drugs had hit the landscape and I embraced my share of "far out" experiences.

I wasn't a complete hedonist. I was there to learn, and found the intellectual climate extremely stimulating. It was the late 1960's and students ruled.

With a major in Political Science, I totally engaged with the political and social events of the day. My childhood plan to become president still simmered on the back burner, along with trying to find ways to make life better for others. I considered a major in Sociology, but the gnawing awareness of the need for political change haunted me, so I stayed with Political Science. All the while, the issues of the 1960's churned society, and I threw myself into the activities of the time. I was definitely a product of my generation, and I loved it.

I volunteered as an academic tutor to help African American kids catch up with their white peers in the newly integrated North Carolina school system, attended SDS (Students for a Democratic Society) meetings, opposed the Viet Nam war, and supported the civil rights and the women's rights movements. I clearly wanted to create a better world. "Make love, not war" and the ideals of the flower children of the 1960's appealed to me.

Depression

Then, at the beginning of my senior year, a deep wave of depression hit me that I was buried under for weeks. I felt myself sinking and my Tom Sawyer optimism drifting away in a hazy mist. Maybe it was too many parties, or too many political issues. Maybe it was the Viet Nam War and all my friends being drafted. The depression was thick and unnerving. I had never asked others for help. I was a loner when it came to handling my personal problems. Usually, my inner dialogue served me well. I could always connect to who I was and use my will power to get out of trouble. This time I couldn't find myself, and it took a massive amount of focus to locate my will power. I was a "thinker" and "analyzer" of life. Thinking about the depression and its horror, I knew I had to break out of it. As an espoused atheist, appealing to God was no option. It didn't even occur to me. I had reveled in the power of myself, so I knew that my will would be my only savior.

But where was I?

Heavy, lost, and alone, I started to will myself out of depression. I was so imploded that I knew that to explode was the only way out, or my life energy would be sucked away forever. But how?

I opened my dormitory window and looked at the stars. All my old friends were there: Orion, Cassiopeia, The Big Dipper, all the constellations I'd bonded with in childhood. They welcomed me into their expansiveness. I knew all about them: the sword on Orion's Belt, Caspar and Pollux of the Gemini twins, Scorpio's fanned tail. My star friends and I had explored the universe together. I spoke a tentative "hello" to my old buddies, and they sparkled, pulling me into their world. I felt a huge energy welling up from deep inside and called louder, "Hello!"

These were my friends. They lived in the expansiveness of the universe while I, on the other hand, was buried in a little hole inside my fear and pain, stuck and lost. They were calling me out! Impulsively, I ran down the stairs and into the cool night. Looking up into the starry eyes of my universe, I yelled out, "Hello." Then louder, "Hello!" ... "Are you still there? Talk to me!

Come and get me! Pull me out of this! I'm here! I love you." I began running like a madwoman all over the rich green campus lawns. I screamed, howled, and bellowed my greetings to the stars, bursting out of my tiny, imploded world.

I continued for hours, forcing my energy into the air around me.

The joy started as a small trickle. As I continued to yell and scream at my star friends, the small trickle grew to a little stream. I jumped and cartwheeled and leaped and fell down, maintaining the flowing frenzy, avoiding going back into that dark hole.

I vocalized until exhausted and breathless, then fell on the ground. When I finally sat up and looked around, it was the middle of the night. But I had won! The depression was shattered in broken pieces all around me. I vowed to never let myself fall into despair again. I keep reaching for life.

The stars are a special gift for me, and my next visit with them was even more profound. I think I know them personally. They invited me into the experience that changed me forever.

"ONE"

Shortly after overcoming that depression, it happened. It came out of the blue, with no intention, desire, or request. It was thrust upon me one day when I took a walk in the country with a friend. It was a gorgeous fall day, the trees golden and the sky a brilliant blue. We decided to lie on our backs in a field and gaze at the sky.

Looking up into the heavens I thought about the stars that were hidden in the immensity of blue. Though I couldn't see them, I knew they were there. I slightly shifted my gaze to look between them and then beyond them, stretching my internal sight to peer as far as I could into the emptiness of space. I waded into empty space farther and farther. I gazed beyond the stars ... and without warning, the emptiness drowned me. It engulfed me. It took me over. It was everywhere. It owned me, became me, dissolved me. I was no longer me. I was everything. I was the air, the light, the field, my friend. I was God, the devil, all love, all pain. I was everything and the nothing in everything. I had no idea how long I lay there. I had slipped between the cracks and would never climb out again.

Eventually, my friend and I stood up. I turned and looked around, in a completely different space, awed by the unity about me, and stunned by the realization that I was One with everything. I was silent for a while, examining the newness of my perceptions.

Finally, I said from a level of innocence I had never known before, "I'm One with you." He looked at me quizzically. "And I'm One with the space between us. You are me, and I am the trees, the earth, and the grass ..." I could tell he didn't get it. I didn't care. I was too consumed by my new recognition of myself as everything. I became silent and a pure subtle joy awoke inside. A deep peace was present. He didn't get it. He didn't have to get it. It was me who got it. So I dropped the subject. It was too new, too fresh, too precious to explain. I said, "I'll see you later," and walked slowly home, feeling that something very big had occurred, but not sure quite what.

That night, before going to bed, I put a sign on my mirror just in case I might forget about what had happened to me that day. It said, "ONE."

Next Morning

Well, there was no way I could forget this experience! It dominated everything in my awareness. I couldn't sleep it off or shake it off! It was as permanent as having fallen into indelible ink. But this ink was clear. It didn't show. Only I knew that I had fallen into the inkwell and was marked for good.

People acted like I was normal. It was weird talking to everyone and being One with them. I liked it. I felt connected to them. It was kind of fun, like knowing a secret that no one else knew. It was so obvious to me, but everyone else was oblivious. Now what? I had no answer, so I focused on my day, stopped thinking about Oneness, and just went to class. But it didn't go away. It followed me everywhere.

It was hard to communicate to people what had happened. Every time I told someone I was One with them, they gave me a strange look and seemed to distance themselves, as if I was getting too familiar. Some people thought I was having a drug experience, but drugs wear off, and this didn't. If I really got into explaining that I was One with them and One with everything, they usually suggested seeing a psychiatrist. So I stopped talking about it. I was trying to figure it out, and soon discovered I'd have to do that on my own.

I wasn't religious, yet now knew that I was God. I wasn't looking for spiritual insights, but every spiritual insight now presented at my fingertips. The idea of being an atheist was a joke. God had just proved Itself to me. I understood Jesus and Buddha, the saints and the scriptures, Plato and Aristotle. It did occur to me that I might be some kind of messiah with all the answers. With that thought, I really knew I'd better keep this a secret!

I couldn't even coherently explain to anyone what had happened. I did know that it was the Truth, and that my experience of it could not be denied.

This experience became the backdrop of everything in my life. I couldn't lose the experience, even when I tried. Trying to lose it became absurd! It was like trying to stay dry in the ocean. It didn't go away.

I liked this experience. I liked knowing that I was Infinite and One with all life. Sometimes I ignored it and pretended to be insignificant and small, afraid and lost, but it was always in the background, as if laughing at me. I couldn't suffer for very long. I realized that it would be ridiculous to kill myself, because I couldn't die. So why not figure out what I was supposed to be doing? That was my biggest challenge, figuring out what to do with all this incredible, unshakeable Oneness.

Chapter 2

The Quest

Was anyone else having the Oneness experience? I mean, anyone living now in my time on earth? I knew Jesus had it because He said, "I and my Father are One," and certainly many philosophers talked about it, but they were all dead.

I'd begun talking about the Oneness as my "Oneness Theory" after receiving such skeptical reactions when trying to describe my experience. So I called it a theory, and found that academia in 1968 was much more receptive to a theory than to an experience. A theory was something we could discuss. I would tell people about my interesting Oneness Theory and ask if they knew anyone having the experience. They introduced me to the writings of many philosophers, poets, and authors, and I eagerly read their works, but still, they were all dead. Was I the only one alive having this experience?

Many people had suggestions about where to find others who might be having the Oneness experience. They sent me to encounter groups, ashrams, and communes. I didn't find anyone. I had developed an elementary Oneness test that would tell me if someone was having the experience. I would look directly and deeply into their eyes without wavering, and if someone could hold my gaze indefinitely, I considered that the proof. I believed that if they could hold my gaze we would connect in our Oneness.

I would go around staring into people's eyes to see if they could hold my gaze. No one could do it. It never occurred to me that it might be a little odd to check people out by peering into their eyes, but I was desperate to find one other person experiencing Oneness with everything. Nothing else was as important! I would go anywhere to find that person.

Love and War

Rick was my first true love. We met in my last year at UNC. He liked my Oneness Theory but we didn't talk about it much. I had learned to just live with it. Rick avoided the Viet Nam war by staying in college as long as possible. His time finally ran out, and he was drafted. I'll never forget the day he left. He walked down the stairs in that crisp khaki soldier uniform, looking so young, beautiful, and innocent, like a child about to run into the backyard to play war with his friends. My world caved in. Seeing him in his soldier uniform, the floor fell out from under me. I felt myself spinning and falling, crashing into the horror of Napalm and rice paddies. "No! Stop!

Run!" I was screaming inside, while on the outside I smiled and turned numb as my lamb walked into the gaping jaws of the hell we had resisted for so long. We rode to the airport in silence, holding hands, squeezing hands, the only way we could communicate our inner desperation without risking hysteria.

Hundreds of other boy-men gathered at the airport. Everyone was drinking; it was a big cocktail party. The din of forced laughter was deafening. I couldn't speak. I just looked into his eyes, with a pleading helpless stare. It was time to go—a kiss, the last hug, his quickly expelled breath pushing the words into my ear, "I'll come back." And then he was gone.

Rick did come back, but our relationship was lost in the jungles of Viet Nam. The horror of that war and my intimate connection to it, I buried deep inside. The pain was too fresh, too raw, still bleeding. I stuffed it down.

This issue would haunt me for many years, compelling me to find a means to heal myself and help this suffering world. Could I somehow use the Oneness to change the world?

Transcendental Meditation

Then I was out of college and living in Boston, working at WBZ, a popular rock and roll radio station, and taking a break from political science. I was hanging around the encounter group/commune crowd, looking for someone experiencing Oneness. My friend, Helen, who knew about my Oneness theory, told me that sometimes when she meditated in a group, she felt at One with everyone present.

Meditation? What's that? I'd better investigate. If there was a chance of people experiencing Oneness there, I had to explore it.

I was off to meditate, something called Transcendental Meditation (TM). On May 2, 1970, I showed up at the TM Center looking for anyone experiencing Oneness. I didn't find one person. Nevertheless, I listened to the lectures and learned the technique. Finally, on the last night of the classes the teacher started talking about Cosmic Consciousness. That was what I was looking for! I raised my hand and asked if he knew anyone experiencing Cosmic Consciousness.

"Oh yes!" he replied. "The founder of TM, Maharishi Mahesh Yogi, is definitely, at the least, in Cosmic Consciousness."

"How can I meet him?" I demanded.

He's training teachers of TM and you can take a course."

I knew that I had to look Maharishi Mahesh Yogi in the eyes. But how would I organize that?

Baba Ram Dass

In the meantime, I actually did meet someone who was experiencing Oneness. Baba Ram Dass, the former Dr. Richard Alpert of LSD fame, was in Boston giving lectures. He had found an Indian spiritual master and was on a whole new life track. He happened to be staying at his family home in New Hampshire the same weekend I was in New Hampshire with a group of friends. I suggested that we go over and meet him. They were lukewarm, but willing. I checked the phone book. He was listed! I made the phone call, asked to see him, and we got the invitation. To my dismay, he was returning to India the very next day, so we had to get over there now!

When our group arrived, I was the only one who got out of the car. "Come on," I called to the others, but no one would join me. I wasn't going to let this opportunity drop because my friends were timid. I marched up to the back door and knocked. Baba Ram Dass opened the door and stepped out.

On the drive over, I had been practicing what to say. I needed a sentence to hold me in the moment, to communicate why I was there. The Infinity of pure Oneness was washing over me, just anticipating a meeting with someone who lived in the Oneness. Looking into his eyes, I uttered the words I had practiced. The best I could come up with was, "I hope you have a pleasant journey back to India," and then I held his gaze. He looked into my eyes for a long time. Everything fell away and we sank into a communion of Oneness. No more words needed to be spoken. We embraced for an eternal silent moment, then bid farewell. I floated back to the car, unaware of my feet touching the ground. It all happened in less than five minutes, but we had united in the Oneness.

Finally, I had found one other living person having the Oneness experience. It had taken me almost two years, and he was leaving the country the next day! I was dismayed that I wouldn't have the chance to hang out with him, talk with him, share thoughts on the Oneness with him. At least I had the assurance that he knew what I was experiencing. He knew the Oneness. I wasn't alone with it anymore.

It took me a year to raise the funds and organize my life to meet another person who was living Oneness.

Maharishi's TM

I liked TM and found that it helped me with everything. I became calmer, more focused, self-confident and productive. What I liked most about TM was Maharishi's plan to make a better world. He explained that if enough people meditated and became peaceful within, the world would be peaceful. I believed he was right. It was about raising people's consciousness. A life purpose started arising. I could see a way to heal the world. Maybe I wouldn't have to become president, after all.

I had tried for years to change people on the outside through social programs and political activism. It was exhausting to shift even one person's thinking. Here was a way for people to change themselves from the inside. I was excited about the possibility of empowering people to grow from within by teaching them how easy it was to contact the Infinite Source of all their thoughts. This would allow them to naturally unfold into creative, productive, and stress-free human beings. It could even be a way to prevent war!

I eagerly anticipated the TM Teacher Training Program. When I arrived for the first stage of the course at the University of Massachusetts in Amherst, Mass., in 1971, I was so ready to meet Maharishi. I was very excited about TM, but my real goal was to look Maharishi in the eyes. If he didn't pass the Oneness test, I was out of there.

Just being at the course with Maharishi was wonderful. His presence was so powerful, it tangibly embraced and carried me to new heights of expansion. This was the power of consciousness he talked about. Everything he said made sense, based upon my Oneness experience, and he explained how Oneness could be given to everyone though TM. I was so excited about the possibility of not being alone in experiencing this anymore. I could become a TM teacher and give the experience to thousands! I was ready to drop everything and teach TM, except for one last item—the Oneness test.

Maharishi and the Oneness Test

Finally, I had my chance to meet Maharishi one-on-one. I had gotten an advanced technique and he was going to meet with each person who had gotten it. I stood in line to walk up and sit with him alone so he could check the advanced technique. I had worn a mini dress that day with a scoop neck and no sleeves. Not exactly what I would have chosen to meet an Indian monk, but this was a spur of the moment meeting, and I had no time to change. Then it was my turn. I walked forward and sat down, trying to cover my knees, but aware that as I pulled the dress over my knees, it pulled the neck too low, so I pulled the neck up and exposed half my thigh. Back and forth it went—adjusting from low neck to high thigh. It was impossible to cover up! I finally stopped trying, turned to him, and took a very long look into his eyes.

The world dropped out from under me. I fell, tumbling into the Infinite. I let go into all my Oneness and plunged into a vast universality. I glimpsed the immense Infinite Life Maharishi was living. I became lost in it, drowning in it. Here was someone who could teach me how to live the Infinite Life. He was living it bigger than anyone I had ever met, read about, or dreamed of. Most certainly he was living it bigger than I was. I broke the gaze. I pulled away, humbled and awed by what he had shown me in his eyes. Silently, internally I signed on with Maharishi.

Teaching TM

I was hooked. Everything I wanted was being offered by Maharishi. I spent the next twenty years teaching TM and its advanced courses, running centers, and organizing projects for Maharishi. I took advanced training courses at least once a year to deepen my experience and receive further knowledge. In the advanced training courses, I spent many hours in deep meditation, balanced by light activity. It gave me a chance to stay in the source of thought, what Maharishi called the Transcendent, which is now called by scientists, the Unified Field—my Oneness place—for long periods of time. Maharishi was available to answer questions and give further guidance. He was very interested in developing our consciousness.

I received my Master's Degree for Research in Consciousness from Maharishi European Research University for the many hours I spent exploring consciousness on the long meditation courses. I studied the ancient Vedic knowledge from which TM originates. I learned how the universe is created, how it expands and evolves. I realized how the unbounded Source manifests itself into form and becomes the expression of all that we experience as relative time and space. I learned how we evolve through relative time and space and grow into unity with our unbounded Source. Maharishi delineated seven states of consciousness through which we can evolve to perceive our unity with everything. My Oneness experience was explained over and over again from different angles, traditions, and scientific research. I grew to embrace the Vedic knowledge because I recognized it in my own experience.

I had found my calling. It felt safe and right and perfect. The knowledge invigorated me. The best part about it was being certain that it was true. I stopped talking about my Oneness and let it Be. Everyone had their own inner experience and I had mine. Everyone was evolving and so was I. That's all that mattered. I was on the fast-track of evolution now and it thrilled me.

I had many friends and deep relationships with other TM teachers. My family became involved. All my siblings became TM teachers and my parents learned to meditate. Even though my father was initially opposed to it, he eventually learned and valued his meditation, never missing a day's practice. He even arranged for some of his employees to learn.

All of us practicing TM lifted the consciousness of our family, and this changed the way we looked at problems and petty squabbles. It unified us on a deep level so we could handle the surface differences without the long-term scars that so many families carry. It really pulled our family together into a strong, powerful unit of support, love, and acceptance.

During this time I met my husband, David, on an advanced TM course. He was a bright, innocent breath of fresh air in my life. He took things lightly and laughed a lot. He wore Hawaiian shirts and was a bit irreverent about spiritual concepts. When I told David about the Oneness he said, "Great, wonderful, no problem. Now let's enjoy it." I looked into his eyes and he held my gaze.

David loved nature and took me on wonderful excursions into the rural areas around his Hastings, Michigan, home. If I got too serious he would grab me, throw me up in the air, and catch me in his arms. His playfulness completely disarmed me. His adventuresome spirit turned me into a child again. David had a full, rich heart and I was struck by the value he placed on love as the force that moves everything in the universe. He gave a much needed balance to my life's intense spiritual focus.

We got married in 1979. David and I had a deep friendship before we ever got married. This friendship has helped us through our share of tough times. It's easy to find a new romance, but it's hard to find a good friend. David gave me both.

David has supported my spiritual work unconditionally, and provided a grounding and stabilizing influence as I explored the inner depths of my heart and soul. With his kind, open, giving, accepting nature, he helped me to uncover the next phase of my life's work.

My years teaching TM were very fulfilling. As the organization spread under Maharishi's guidance, it eventually grew to include many millions of people world-wide practicing TM. I felt a part of something big, something that was changing the world.

Initially my search was for someone else having the Oneness experience. I had found Maharishi, and he opened the depth of internal wealth that my Oneness experience offered. For a long time, I was content with this as I studied and learned and applied his teachings, not knowing that something more was growing from it that would catapult me into the lap of Divine Mother.

Chapter 3

Devotion

What about God?

A conflict was growing within. The more I meditated, the more I learned, and the more my appreciation of the Grand Architect of the universe grew. I was becoming an ardent devotee of God. This surprised me! TM is not a religion, but I was having religious feelings.

Maharishi often talked about how TM can awaken our spiritual life. He had also encouraged scientific research on TM. Now, more and more research came out verifying its good effects on the body. So we offered TM as a systematic technique to release stress. As a TM teacher, I talked at length about the research and the release of stress. A huge body of scientific knowledge had been published about the Transcendental Meditation Program® and its positive effects on mental clarity, social behavior, health, and world peace. I presented TM in this scientific language. I explained the scientific charts. I honored the scientific path. But within me surged a tremendous wave of pure devotional energy that I could not repress. I wanted to talk about God. I became steeped in deep devotion to the Divine Intelligence that made all this science possible. My heart was breaking open with devotion, yet I felt confined to discussing spirituality in terms of releasing stress.

I sensed that there was more than meditation, a life with the Divine that I hadn't yet touched. My Christian religion hadn't given it to me. My meditation organization didn't talk about it. I was One with everything, but where was God? The experience of Pure Being wasn't satisfying my hunger to engage in a personal relationship with God. I yearned to reach out and shake hands with God. Maharishi had said it was possible, and I believed him.

I found myself thinking about God all the time. More than that, love exploded in my inner life for the Supreme Being. I wanted to talk to God. I wanted to find the Creator and have a discussion with Him. It became an intensely passionate drive. It had been ten years since God had proven Its existence as abstract Oneness permeating my whole life. Now I needed the personal relationship. Love was overflowing, spilling out of my heart. In those ten years, I had gone from stark atheist to ardent devotee. But where was God, the Beloved?

My Search for God

Continuing to teach TM full-time, I began trying to find my way to this personal relationship with the Divine. I searched through many religious teachings and philosophies. I read books, went to self-development lectures, studied the Bible, went to church, and asked Jesus Christ. I prayed.

At this point, I was experiencing a spiritual crisis. I had been completely content in my Self as One with everything, but now my heart was looking for further expansion so its love could flow bigger. I was being pulled out of where I had been into a more cosmic experience of love.

I loved Maharishi and for many years was completely devoted to his work, but now I was experiencing a larger calling, to love something more than a human being who embodies Divinity, but instead to love the Divinity itself.

In his book, *The Science of Being and the Art of Living*, Maharishi discusses the personal and impersonal aspects of God. The impersonal aspect is the Unified Field, the Oneness. He also emphasizes that we can develop a state of consciousness in which we can meet and communicate with a personal God. So now, with the Oneness established, how to get to the personal aspect of God? I had to have it!

So I started seeking God in the traditional church of my childhood. I spoke with the Episcopal Minister at my hometown parish. It was evident that his experience did not embrace the Oneness. He didn't understand the Love that was compelling me to reach into this Oneness to find a Divine form originating from it. Again, I felt isolated and left to my own devices.

I read the Christian scriptures. It seemed Jesus must have been unified with God. Wanting the Truth from the Source, I focused on His statements rather than the reports on what He did. It became clear to me that Jesus knew the Oneness. From my perspective, His statement, "I and my Father are One," clearly referred to his experience of Oneness. This was His core teaching. He was talking about His experience, not a philosophy. That was great, I understood that.

So Jesus was experiencing Oneness with God like I was, but He also seemed to have a relationship with God as a Divine Person, a "Father." My relationship with God was as Pure Being, abstract and impersonal. I couldn't talk to Pure Being. Where was the "person" of God? When I would pray to my "Father in Heaven," I got nothing, no response, no feeling of a relationship. He didn't talk back. I could rattle off the Lord's Prayer because I had memorized it. I never heard a response. I wanted a conversation. Jesus had the conversation. We both knew we were One with God, but He had something more, a lot more. He could hear God. I wanted what He had.

I investigated other churches, looking for one that honored all religions and paths to God. Since I was experiencing Oneness with everything, I could not commit to any religion that did not honor my experience.

I explored Hinduism and Buddhism because they teach that we are all One. But at the same time, I wasn't comfortable abandoning my own tradition—I wanted to give Christianity another chance here. I reasoned that if Christianity had lasted for so long, it must hold somewhere within it the Truth that all are One. Jesus lived it and taught it, but His churches weren't telling people about it.

I looked into what it would take to become an ordained minister, first in the Episcopal Church, my family's denomination, but then also, in the Unity Church, because it acknowledged all paths to God. I chose to join the Unity Church.

But it wasn't enough just to join a church. I still hadn't found the experience I was longing for. I had to meet God face to face. But how?

I was used to running my thoughts by Maharishi and getting a response. I would have liked to ask him for personal guidance in this, but over the years, he had become less and less available to TM teachers in the field. I had no access to him. He was cloistered at his international center in The Netherlands. The administrators of the organization could see him and report on what he advised, but I missed the direct communication. If Maharishi wasn't available to answer my questions, I had to find another way to get answers. I had to talk directly to God.

A Leap of Faith

"The Kingdom of Heaven is within you." Maharishi had repeated these famous words many times. The same message had come from Jesus and many other spiritual Masters. This was a common link in the teachings of these enlightened individuals.

I decided to take the Kingdom of Heaven statement literally, and look within me. I would go on a search for Heaven within me, within the Oneness. I resolved to stop attending lectures, reading books, taking seminars, or doing anything else that took my attention to other people's version of "Heaven."

I had been looking outside myself to find Heaven "out there" in the words and experiences of others. Where was this elusive Heaven? What does it mean, "Heaven is within you"? To me, "Heaven" meant meeting God face to face, getting to know Him, and having a personal relationship with the Supreme Being. I had questions to ask, answers to get. I wanted an ongoing dialogue with God. Oneness is great, but I couldn't talk to it. I had Pure Being, now I needed the Supreme Being.

The first conscious act of faith that I ever took in my life was to believe Maharishi and Jesus when they said that the Kingdom of Heaven is within. I wanted that kingdom. I sensed a treasure. I had no map to it, but I felt its nearness. Looking within was a key that I had to use to unlock what was waiting for me. I would plunge into myself and search for it.

The Kingdom of Heaven

It was 1986, and I now had an infant daughter. While she took her nap every afternoon, I looked for the Kingdom of Heaven.

Closing my eyes, I took my first few awkward steps.

"Where is the Kingdom of Heaven?" my inner voice whispered. It was dark, nothing was happening.

"Where is the Kingdom of Heaven?" No response. More darkness.

Hmm … this is boring … "Is anybody home? …"

Silence.

"Jesus … Mother Mary … God?"

No Response.

… Sigh …

"This is going to be a long afternoon."

I looked around inside in the darkness, and found nothing but more darkness.

"I'm not giving up," I said firmly. "I've read books by enlightened sages, gone to lectures on inner development, studied Christian, Buddhist, and Vedic scriptures, and they all say the power is inside. Where? I'm sick of hearing about other people's experiences of God, I want my own. I've been told that Heaven can be here and now, not in some afterlife, so show it to me!"

I was getting demanding …

I took a deep breath …

I settled down a little …

Whew …

I called inwardly, "Help me! I'm looking for the Kingdom of Heaven!"

Blank wall …

Nothingness …

Day after day this went on, darkness and more darkness. I was not going to quit until I found Heaven or discovered its non-existence. After about a month, this discipline became part of my routine. I didn't tell anyone, not even my husband, what I was doing. Finding Heaven was my private project and if I failed no one would know.

Light within Darkness

Days and weeks passed. I lost track of time.

I was quite used to the darkness by now. It was soothing, and deep. I kept asking to be shown Heaven, but not as often anymore, not as insistently. The darkness was comforting, safe, familiar … I was relaxing, but would anything ever happen?

"What am I doing here anyway? Is this going anywhere?" Self-doubt nagged me.

"Why am I doing this? Maybe there is no Kingdom of Heaven."

Something flickered in my awareness …

Hmmm …

What's that?

Another flicker …

A light? …

I lost it …

What's the use? …

There it is again …

Gone again …

I took a deep breath …

Stopped looking for it …

There … it's come back.

A flicker of light.

I stopped straining to see. I had been jumping on it with my mind, and it always went away when I did that. As I let go of trying, the light reappeared.

The light danced before me …

I watched …

It played …

I followed its movement …

Something was happening! An event in the darkness of my inner world!

I examined the light, watched it flicker and flow, changing into many different shapes. It grew, it shrank, it sparkled. Unlike the silent darkness, it was busy!

I watched …

Examined its motion …

Observed …

I got to know the light.

Now, every day in my quest for Heaven, I studied light in my inner awareness. I learned about its qualities, the way it moves and expands, how it breaks up into pieces and disappears, its different shades and intensities. I noticed its freedom to build and change, combine and flow. Light fascinated me and I eagerly anticipated my periods of investigating light each day.

At first, I thought it was the light on the inside of my eyelids, after-images from external light, but after a while it didn't matter. It had a life of its own, and was teaching me about itself.

All this was intriguing, but even better was the way it made me feel. My body felt freer, enlivened. I felt lighter in weight, expansive, released from everyday problems.

Then the light started to interact with me! It started to flow into and through me, opening me deeper into more light. Light cascaded through me, and I was changing day by day.

Everything in my life got better. Light could lift me out of a bad mood. I could be angry and stressed, go inside to do my Heaven research, and light would transform my negativity. I didn't call this light "Heaven." No God or angel came to me, but it was definitely a sign to keep going. In fact, as I would later discover, it became a tool to get to Heaven.

I had been sitting in the dark for weeks and finally someone had rolled me a flashlight!

Light Communicates

Light wanted to communicate with me, I was sure of that. It was showing me the inner world I had entered. I couldn't understand its language, but knew that it was teaching me. Light was intelligent! Light guided me every day now in my Heaven research. It wanted to be known.

Each day I would invite it. I would start by saying out loud, "Divine Light is filling me now. Divine Light is flooding me now, pouring into me." My voice got softer as I spoke until I was saying the words inwardly. I called it "Divine" Light because it made me feel so good. It made me feel that I was approaching Heaven, and that by following this Divine clue, it would take me to Heaven. It was as if someone was dropping bread crumbs for me to follow, only these were "Light crumbs."

"Divine Light is filling me now." As I said the words, the Light would start flowing in. If

I was angry or distressed, it took longer to get it going. It first had to push the negative energy away. Eventually Light appeared, and I would be changed, feeling significantly better, lighter, and happier.

I used the Light every time I felt bad or "off." It was healing me. It worked so well that I started using it on David, and even my little daughter. When David was irritable, I said the words silently. I knew he was filling with Light, and he responded well. His demeanor changed. I tried it on friends who were disturbed and upset, and they shifted for the better. The Light was definitely impacting others' dispositions.

I put together a way to dissolve my negative moods by repeating in words what the Light was doing in me. I watched the Light and whatever it did, I verbalized. "Divine Light is filling me now. Divine Light is flooding me now. Divine Light is increasing in me again and again. It is pouring into me." I didn't realize it then, but I was translating the motion of Light into English words. Whatever Light did on a vibrational level, I would say in English words. I called it a "prayer" because I was using it to bring myself and others closer to Heaven, though it was unlike any prayer I had ever heard of.

This unusual "prayer" went on for several minutes describing what Divine Light did as I watched it. I was now using this "prayer" for many people in my life. I used it on people I didn't get along with or for a meeting I was dreading, and the Light improved them! Soon I was pouring Divine Light all over the difficult people and problem situations I encountered.

I originally created this "prayer" based on Divine Light's presentation within me. I have learned now that others can say these same words describing the activity of Divine Light, and Light starts to respond to the words for them. By calling in "Divine Light," anyone can cause Light to increase and flow within them.

Though I didn't know it at the time, this was my first experience of translating the Divine language into verbal expression.

Back in my Heaven research, I used this Light to heal myself every day. I discovered that Light had the ability to release stuck places in my system. I could sense these blockages as heavy, dense, or agitated areas. As I focused there and poured the Light into them by saying or thinking the "prayer," the emotion or heaviness changed. I became lighter, freer, and able to see my situation from a larger perspective.

Divine Love from Divine Light

Then something wondrous began to happen. As I worked with Light, I noticed a new quality starting to appear. My heart engaged with the Light, and as it dissolved heavy energies and negative emotions, my heart opened more. I liked it. I felt warmth and comfort, happiness and a quiet peace with a lively vitality. My inner focus shifted to this wonderful experience. I stopped watching Light and examined this new phenomenon. When I gave it my full attention, it opened up to me and drew me in. I began filling with a quality that felt like love. Could it be love? Could it be Divine Love? Had Divine Light led me to Divine Love?

This was astounding. There was no reason for me to be filling with love; nothing had caused its expression. It was just there, filling me more and more. It was the *energy* of love, not an emotion. My mind didn't understand it, but my heart fully engaged in opening to it. At that moment, I had no object to love, no person to love, no reason to love, but here was love moving, opening, and saturating me. Is it possible for love to be energy, pure and simple on its own? This kind of love I needed to learn more about.

I studied Divine Love as intensively as I had researched Divine Light. I noticed first that it was all about my heart. This energy drew my attention to my heart, and my heart expanded, enriched, and all my senses awakened to it. My logical mind could not fathom Divine Love. Its mere presence sent my thinking mind into a frustrating search for a definition of love. But no mental definition was ever enough. How could I be experiencing so much love without an object to love? I was just sitting in it, immersed in it. Pure love was present now without any purpose except to increase itself. All love wanted was more love. The more I allowed it, the more it filled me.

Now, when I went into my inner world, Divine Love permeated my experience, and drew me into something beyond anything I had ever known in the outer world. It kept pulling me into its core. Its allure was all encompassing, and I was compelled to follow, like a lost traveler exhausted and alone, following a distant light to a warm hearth and soft bed. Divine Love was supremely attractive, and it released all my fears.

I created the Divine Love "prayer" as I had created the Divine Light "prayer," by describing my experience with it. I started healing myself and others with this extraordinary energy. I had discovered another way to dismantle negative influences.

I realized years later that, in these "prayers," I had created structures through which Divine Energy could flow. The structures were composed of words, sentences, grammar, and punctuation, and something more important—my *attention*.

I was learning to focus my attention on Divine Qualities, first Light and then Love, and each Divine Quality was flying like an arrow to wherever my attention aimed it, to my problems, my fears, or other people's negativity. Wherever it was aimed, it dissolved the problem and opened me to a creative serenity.

Chapter 4

Turning Point

Divine Light and now Divine Love were changing my experience of life. My thinking mind was letting go of control as Light and Love dominated my inner focus. I couldn't understand either one mentally, but my heart understood, and I began looking to my heart for guidance.

This was a turning point. It was prompted by my encounter with Divine Love. Now when I went inside to do my daily research, I would focus on what was happening in my heart, and my heart was going through major transformation! Using the power of Divine Love, I investigated the inner workings of my heart.

A Constricted Heart

I started to notice that my heart had been constricted for a long time, and felt like it was suffocating. In the past I had ignored it, as most people do, to just get on with life. But now my heart wouldn't let me ignore it anymore. Being a dominantly mental person, I could function well by sneaking past the knots in my heart, and going into my mind. I needed a way to break my heart free of the mental dominance that had restricted its ability to express fully. My mind had captured my heart and put it in a cage. My heart needed to break out so I could be me, the real me.

Insights came about how I had pushed my heart aside repeatedly and let my mind lead. Most of my intuitions, I had negated with my mind, only to find out later that the intuitions were correct.

Often, I held back love because the mind judged it as being irrelevant, or I was embarrassed to allow its innocence to express honestly. I had mostly controlled myself, ignoring or denying the tendencies of my heart for fear of becoming too vulnerable and exposed. There was pain in my heart. I had restricted my heart for so long that the pain had grown into a deep ache begging for release. My heart was desperate for freedom.

I spontaneously breathed into it. Again, I took a deep breath into my heart, like the gasp of a drowning person finally surfacing for air. My heart was suffering under the pressure of my mind's opinions of it. These opinions came from cultural beliefs that the intellect was superior to emotions: "If the emotions come from the heart, then lock the heart in a box; don't let it out in public. Live in your head and never let the heart express, lest you be found to be a fool." I had bought into this philosophy simply to be accepted by others.

I had a lot more to express, but had stifled it most of my life. As a teenager, I had even developed a rash on my chest and neck whenever I held back my emotions, or was intensely nervous about something. The power in my heart scared me when it unexpectedly escaped in a fit of rage, grief, or passion. I was afraid this power could get out of control if I didn't keep a tight rein on it. Now, the pressure had built up and needed release.

I breathed into my heart again to ease the pain of the pressure. The more I breathed into it, the more the pressure released. The currents of breath moving into my heart began to dissolve layers of pent-up intensity. As one level of pain released, another appeared, so I breathed into that, easing away each knot of pain with the streams of breath. I was amazed to experience the pressure and pain dissolving. But then another knot would be revealed, so I breathed into that. Every time one level of pain dissolved, another came up. Each pain that came up had a different feel and flavor, but I recognized each as a blockage to be healed.

Since I was experiencing the Oneness and had been meditating for many years, I was surprised to find there was pain in my heart. It appeared now that all the progress I was making could not continue until I went into my heart to face these blockages holding my hidden issues. Divine Love had brought me here. Where was it taking me now?

I continued breathing into my heart, and finally Light appeared and space opened up. I breathed into that. It deepened, and expanded. Knots of pain were still dissolving but the peaceful space grew until it finally dominated my awareness. Light accompanied the peace, and I breathed into the Light, only to discover more Light and expansion.

Now I was in the realm of something new. The pressure and pain were gone, yet something was there. I kept breathing into it. My old friend Light was shining through with lots of expansion. I breathed into the Light, and experienced more Light and deeper expansion. Now I was getting somewhere! Was this the Kingdom of Heaven? Lots of Light, lots of expansion and peace … sure felt good. The whole process had taken twenty to thirty minutes and I was transformed. My heart felt freed.

Healing My Heart

This was the beginning of my heart's healing. I became very consistent about checking to see if my heart was free of constriction and pressure before I started my inner research. When it was clear, I could better perceive what was going on within me.

This "heart exercise" using the breath, was so effective, I could not confine it to my periods of inner research. When anxiety and worries seized me during the day, I immediately shifted attention to my heart, and breathed into it until they subsided. I started using this to center myself anytime.

I remember getting a distressing letter in the mail just before leaving home. As I drove off, I could feel the pain and pressure in my chest. I started breathing into it and by the time I got to my destination, it had dissipated.

Anytime I was afraid, panicked, disappointed, or angry, I breathed into my heart. I did it waiting for a doctor's appointment, when I couldn't sleep, or when family members upset me.

It even worked on other people. Once, taking a walk with my husband, he began complaining angrily about a situation at work. I felt his tension and anguish, so I started breathing into my heart. In less than a minute he said, "That really doesn't matter right now. Let's enjoy our walk." We both laughed and everything lightened up.

The Heart as Teacher

Again and again, I practiced breathing into my heart, training my attention to focus there. As my heart relaxed and stepped out of hiding, it taught me things. Now my inner education began in earnest. By connecting to my heart, I found my inner teacher. I was being taught from within! I didn't know how it was happening, but I began getting intuitions and information from my heart.

Questions were answered. Knowledge came. It usually had to do with my life and the decisions I was making as a mother, wife, friend, or teacher. Choices became clear to me. Anything I wanted to know became available when I looked into my heart, like how to handle a sticky situation in the family, or help a troubled friend. Sometimes access to my heart was blocked. I couldn't get in. By breathing into the block, I could dissolve it.

This process of using my heart rather than my head honed my integrity. My heart wouldn't allow me to hide or to evade the truth. It would feel more uncomfortable to hold back my deep feelings and thoughts than to go ahead and tell the truth.

Sometimes this new level of openness was scary, but it always worked out for the best. I remember hesitating to ask a question or give my opinion for fear of seeming stupid. I discovered that just coming out with it made me feel validated, relaxed, and centered, and I got the information I needed. The results were always positive.

As I consistently breathed into my heart, it became a powerful center of amazing information. I started using my heart as a resource for how to live my life.

Messages from God

Around this time, Dr. Peter Meyer, co-author of *Being a Christ* and his student, Rich Bell, came to town to teach some classes. Part of what they taught was how to speak to Divine Beings. Their emphasis was on receiving communication from Divine Beings by focusing on the heart. The heart was my focus, too. I was on the right track!

These classes really gave a boost to my experience. They clarified two things. First, healing is necessary in order to be clear enough to talk to a Divine Being. No wonder I was being given all these Healing Tools.

Second, they provided a test to determine whether you were actually connected to a Divine Being. The test was that once the connection was made, you then asked an important question to authenticate that it truly was a Divine Being. The question was, "Do you come in the name of the Christ?" According to Peter, only true Divine Beings recognizing their Oneness with God can answer "Yes" to that question. If the answer was "No," there was a method for lovingly sending the entity on to a place of healing and further evolution.

Later, I changed the question to "Do you come in the name of God?" I wanted to embrace all spiritual traditions in my authentication check. Either question is very effective and an important safety check in this kind of communication.

I practiced with the group and began to get better at embracing the Divine Connection. I worked with them for a time and received some beautiful Divine messages with them. The class really fueled my engines. It gave me the foundation for the next stage of my journey.

On My Own Again

When our family moved to another state, I lost touch with this group and again was left to my own devices. Somewhat dismayed about leaving them, I wondered if I could continue on my own, but I had to try. I used what I had learned and went forward.

Now, as I examined my heart, I asked for a message. When nothing happened, I asked Jesus Christ to help me.

The first time I silently said the name "Jesus Christ," a huge Light flowed into my heart. Was Jesus really there? I opened to the possibility.

I asked, "Are you Jesus?" The Light increased.

"Are you really Jesus?" More Light, very bright.

"I really want to know if you are Jesus!" Intense Light.

"Wow! What's going on? Is this really Jesus Christ?" The glow of Light increased.

"What do you have to say?" More Light engulfed me with the distinct knowing that He was saying, "I love you."

This was too much for my rational mind to handle, in spite of my experiences with the group. My doubts came forward, and the thought came, "I can't talk to Jesus!"

And the whole thing shut down. I lost the Light. I lost the feeling of Love. It was gone. My doubting mind had closed it out.

The next day I tried again. I prepared by using the Tools I had: bringing in the Light, pouring in the Love, and breathing into my heart for several minutes to clear mental doubts.

The Light came back. The feeling of tremendous Love came back. I had to ignore my mind's tendency to discount experiences that weren't logical. I had to ignore all the years of learning that I am unworthy in the eyes of God, and other such teachings from the Christian Church. I really was beginning to talk to God, or at least Jesus. And didn't He say He was One with God? Am I really beginning to talk to God in the form of Jesus? I needed to find out.

From then on, every day I would talk with Jesus, asking, "Jesus, are you there? Come forth …"

Often I had to heal blocks to talking with Him if He didn't come right away, so I used Divine Light and Divine Love, along with healing methods from Peter and Rich's courses.

And yes! Jesus was starting to talk with me …

And He loved me.

This was fantastic! I now had a Divine Friend. He could take me to the Kingdom of Heaven within! Jesus became my guide. Every time I went into my inner world, I called forth Jesus. I asked Jesus everything: how to pay the bills, raise my child, get along with difficult people.

Whenever I was unsure whether my messages were really coming from Jesus, or if I was just making them up, I asked the authentication question, "Do you come in the name of God." I was learning to discern the vibration of the Divine Presence, whether it was Jesus, Mother Mary, or another. My discernment skills were being developed.

Discernment Skills

I became vigilant about testing the authenticity of every internal message. I learned from my own experience that the human ego-mind can override the Truth of the heart and say "Yes, I come in the name of God" if it is invested in a particular response. I realized that it is necessary to become very cautious, clear, and alert to the impulses in the heart, and to silence the small mind to get a true answer.

I was already familiar with the process of listening to the impulses of my heart. I found that by using the "Heart Exercise," I could stay in my heart, and by using my Divine "Prayer" Tools, I could clear my mind. Then, after asking the authentication question, I would ask my personal question and get the answer from my heart. Then I would again ask the authentication question to affirm the answer was coming in the name of God. I still use this method and find that it is quite reliable.

Over time, I have learned other methods for discerning a Divine voice. True Divine Beings consider us One with them and speak to us as equals, and at the same time they help us to accept ourselves as Divine. There is no trace of ego. They do not criticize us or put us down. They want to help us to recognize our union with God. The experience of their presence is the experience of Love. We feel lifted, energized, and joyful by connecting with a True Divine Being. It is a very powerful and profound experience to be in the Presence of Divinity. These are some of the indications in the experience of receiving a message that will tell you that you are indeed speaking to a Divine Being.

Divine Tools for Everyday Life

Over the next ten years, our son was born and our family moved four times. I was a busy working mother with all kinds of challenges. Late at night after everyone went to bed, I would sit alone in the living room and run my problems by Jesus. Sometimes Mother Mary or Archangel Michael would come.

I got the answers I needed to carry on. During those years, my inner life grew and deepened. I talked to no one about this. My friendship with Jesus and the Divine Beings was something I held inside.

I really didn't know how much Jesus was teaching me then, but now I realize that He cultivated my inner life in those early days. We just kept talking about my daily challenges of being a wife and mother. Often He woke me up during the night to teach me something. My heart was becoming more awake, more healed, and I kept asking questions.

Throughout this time, I was honing the "prayer" tools with my family. If someone was being negative, I started breathing into my heart, with the intention of including their heart, so that I was breathing into both our hearts. Sure enough, the intensity softened, opinions could be expressed without animosity, and harmony was re-established in the home.

Other times when there was discord in the household, I might be washing the dishes and silently saying to an agitated family member, "Divine Light is filling you now. Everyone is filled with Divine Light." If an argument escalated in intensity, I would go somewhere alone for a few minutes to really focus my attention, and clear the abrasive energy with another Tool that I was developing. It involved telling discordant energies to go by saying, "Go! Go into the Light!" It cleared the disturbance, and the household was restored to peace.

I always surrounded my children with Light when I was worried about them. As they became teenagers with more independence and more choices to make, my worries increased. So I continued surrounding them with Light whenever they were out late, hadn't come home on time, went on road trips, or anything else that concerned me for their safety. This practice has continued to deliver them home without mishap. Not only did it protect them, but it calmed me. I will probably be surrounding them with Light for the rest of my life.

As these Tools proved themselves to be highly effective and efficient at releasing negative energies, I started to share them with family members and close friends. I began telling them about my discussions with Jesus and the Divine Group. They wanted to hear more, and to ask questions themselves. I agreed and they asked their questions. I gave them the answers from my Divine Friends. They liked everything about it, felt it was profound, and encouraged me to offer it more widely.

Chapter 5

Discovering Divine Mother

Going Public

My inner experience and relationship with God was the most personal part of my life. I was reluctant to share it with anyone but a trusted inner circle of friends. However, there was an incessant urge from inside pushing me to show others what I was learning. My family and friends were my "guinea pigs." I practiced for years on them and learned how to read their energy, stay in the Light, and bring the wisdom out of my heart. Now they started urging me to share my work more widely.

Even the Divine Gang was prompting me to get it out there. They were saying, "Let us talk to more people and help them with their troubles." I hesitated, hemmed and hawed, afraid of public judgment. I felt a pressure building within as I resisted their prompts. It became very uncomfortable to keep saying "no." Finally, I mustered up the courage to offer the Tools and Divine messages publicly.

Very timidly, I put an ad in the classified section of our local paper simply saying: "Prayer Assistance" and listed my phone number. Three people called, and it grew quickly from there by word of mouth. My life changed dramatically.

New Career—New Challenges

It had been thirteen years since I first started looking for the Kingdom of Heaven. I had discovered some healing methods and a way to talk to God. When I went public, it all really took off. I became so busy that I had to create an organization, which I called Transformational Prayer®. This has now become Divine Mother Guidance and Healing. At first, I called what I did "prayer." As time went on, I realized that these techniques were unlike any other kind of "prayer," and the name confused people, so I started calling them "Energy Healing Tools."

As I continued to use these Tools with many people, I came to recognize that the pain and suffering we humans carry inside is immense. As time went on, however, I found that the Tools and techniques transformed the pain and suffering. People became clear and light. The Tools could lift them out of dense places, and heal the deep pain of unworthiness, guilt, shame, fear, and many other conditions that cause mental anguish, emotional distress, and physical illness.

From having watched Divine Light inside me for so long, my subtle senses had sharpened.

I could now perceive what the subtle energy was doing within a person's system. I started to intuitively see, feel, and know where their energy was blocked, agitated, or stuck in a loop. I perceived dark patches, solid walls, snake-like strands, dense fields, broken connections, and many other unnatural configurations. With every new situation, I would ask my Divine Friends how to clear it.

I had learned how to connect with many Divine Beings by then and they were guiding me. We developed an internal dialogue. One of them, usually Jesus, would come forth to give the instructions. He told me what to do and what steps to take to heal the person. Sometimes it came as a visual impulse, other times as an intuition, often as a physical sensation, but I always got guidance. It was a vibrational language that I learned to understand. After checking to make sure it came in the name of God, I used the methods as instructed. It was amazing how quickly it dissolved the energetic disturbances. At first, I simply spoke the Tools and exercises out loud. Those methods were later written down and are now the printed Divine Mother Healing Tools.

I discovered that each troublesome life issue a person wants to heal has a corresponding energy configuration in that person's system. Usually the condition is layered. Starting to heal it on the surface level, I would then go deeper and deeper into their energy field, rooting out the deepest layers of the problem. Sometimes it would take several sessions to get to the core of a deep, painful concern. Some issues would then steer me into another problem that was more primal. Often, the condition I was healing originated in former lifetimes and had been brought to this lifetime to heal.

Wherever the condition took me I would go after it, taking my Divine Friends with me. They were the ones doing the healing; I was just using my focused attention and healing intention as a doorway for the Divine Energy to flow through. We were colleagues, partners in this marvelous healing process. I held the door open and they poured through with the Love and Light and power capable of transforming the deepest pain.

Divine Grace

One of the most beautiful experiences I had was to discover the Divine Grace Tool. This Tool grew out of the combination of Divine Love and Divine Light. Working with these two qualities so frequently, I eventually experienced them merge and become another distinct quality. This quality drew me into a new inner dimension. It was a sublime and perfect place that went beyond everything I'd experienced or witnessed before. It conveyed perfection beyond anything my mind could imagine. The only name I could use for it was Divine Grace.

One day when I was using the Healing Tools for a man with prostate cancer, the sense of Divine Grace filled me. I found myself repeating aloud, "Divine Grace is filling you. Divine Grace is pouring into you," and I began shifting into that new level of reality.

It struck me that Divine Grace activated a process that could create only the highest and best. At that moment, Divine Grace was creating exactly what this man needed: a healthy prostate gland.

I felt that in this new level of reality, Divine Grace was instantly healing him. In fact, in this reality, the man had never been ill. Now Divine Grace was pouring into him, reminding the cells of his body that he was not sick.

I kept repeating the phrases describing the activities of Divine Grace, and experienced a certainty that he was being healed, and that whatever had caused the illness didn't matter at all. Divine Grace was simply taking over to give him the blessing of health, a blessing he could receive because, from the perspective of Divine Grace, he was not sick. In this dimension of Divine Grace, both my Divine Friends and I were experiencing him as being perfectly healthy.

This was a revelation. It made me realize that there is a place within us that is always perfectly healthy. If we can access and accept that level, illness cannot take hold in our bodies. It is a matter of more powerful laws of nature taking over from less powerful laws of nature. The more powerful laws are more closely aligned with the Divine Truth of our perfection, that we are "made in the image of God." The level of Divine Grace appears to be more fundamental, more universal, and so its nature is to transform all levels of space and time into Divine perfection. Could this be what healing is really all about, remembering our Divine perfection?

Divine Grace was showing this man's body how to function at a more powerful, unified level, where good health was completely stable.

As I continued working with him, I was convinced that this man was healed, yet I still perceived the subtle presence of illness on the surface. I kept saying the words of the Divine Grace Tool that shifted the energy into the level of Divine Grace, where he was already healthy. Then I, as One with the Divine, allowed the level of perfect health to flow into the level of his physical body and transform it. Afterwards, I advised him to continue every day to think or speak out phrases that described Divine Grace filling him, and to image this happening in his life. I believed that this would open the dimension of Divine Grace to his body, causing the scales to eventually tip toward stabilizing the template of perfect health.

Everyone contains the template of perfect health for their body, but in most cases, it has been dormant. Divine Grace wakes up this template so that the body can express it.

Divine Tools and Clearing Tools

As I worked with Love, Light, and Grace, more Tools were revealed from within. Because most people believe they are separate from God, the Tool of Divine Truth came forth next to transform that error belief.

Divine Truth acknowledges that we are One with God and dissolves the untruth of separation from God. As I used the Divine Truth Tool, I perceived within me people's belief structures and fears collapsing like a building being demolished. The fear, shame, and unworthiness and everything created by them, are the structures of untruth in our systems. Divine Truth, embraced energetically, creates an environment within our system that begins reorganizing our physiology to accept the Truth of our Divine Nature, including the Divine Template of our perfect health. In our True Divine Nature, we are not afraid, not ashamed, not unworthy, not ill.

Soon another Tool was revealed. The Ascending Light Healing Tool activates the upward flow of Light in our systems. It raises us into the frequency of Light that transforms the material body into a Divine vessel for us to inhabit.

By now, more people were coming to me, presenting a wide range of challenges. My Divine Friends never let me down, and continued to present more Healing Tools for dealing with every new situation.

To specifically address certain mental and emotional obstructions in my clients' energy systems, I was given the Calling Back Parts Tool for those who have given up their personal power and "lost" pieces of themselves. The Releasing Agreements Tool is for dissolving past contracts and vows that no longer serve one's present situation. The Break Command clears subtle energy structures that confine people's energy to restrictive vibrational patterns. The beautiful Self-Love Exercise, practiced over time, dissolves the pain of unworthiness and low self-esteem. Through my Divine connection, I found myself being given an entire toolkit of vibrational methods to heal many causes of suffering.

I now had two kinds of Tools to dissolve discordant energies and bring people back into connection with their Divine Self: first, the Clearing Tools, to release specific types of discord; and second, the Divine Tools, which filled them with Divine qualities and empowered their Divine Nature. I continued to receive more tools as world conditions changed and new needs presented in the people who came to me.

The Healing Tools had been presented to me one at a time. Now I was using all of them together to heal people's issues and connect them to their Divine Self. I was guided to organize the Tools in a specific order to maximize the healing flow of energy they created. The sequence allowed each Tool to support the others as the unique healing quality of each Divine vibration enabled the next Tool to provide even more purification of the energy field. The Divine Tools and the Clearing Tools worked beautifully together to bring the energy system and physical body into a Divine balance. This powerful energy activation brought people into closer connection with their Divine Self while dissolving the issues afflicting their lives. It was exciting and gratifying to see people change and heal.

Working with Divine Beings

For several years, I worked with Divine Energy mainly using Jesus as my primary connection. I had learned through my meditation practice to allow my attention to move through subtler and subtler layers of inner life until it settled into the Source of Creation, the Unified Field, from where all things manifest. I then investigated the Home of the Divine, what I called "The Kingdom of Heaven," where pure Being first expresses as a form. That is the level where the impersonal God reveals Itself as a personal form of God.

Jesus is a familiar form of God from my own spiritual tradition. I knew there were other forms of the personal God in various spiritual traditions. I also knew there were Archangels and great teachers who had unified with God and had become recognized as God-Beings. I tried to get in contact with them the same way I connected with Jesus. I was amazed to find that they responded with joyful, loving encouragement for me to continue receiving knowledge this way. Jesus appeared to be introducing me to more of his Friends.

Over the years, I became very comfortable with putting my attention on this subtlest level where the Creation is manifesting into form. I learned to focus there, soften into it and allow the flow of the un-manifest Source to answer any question I was posing. I constantly came back to the unbounded Source, and then moved my attention into the subtlest level of form, where the personal presence of God resides. Receiving these messages became so natural that I added this process to my healing methodology.

After going through the sequence of Healing Tools, I would request a message for my clients. I would ask which Divine Being wanted to speak to them. It was often Jesus Christ, Archangel Michael, Mother Mary, or Lord Ram, but others would come depending on the person's Divine affiliations. The Divine Wisdom that came healed and opened their hearts, connected them to their Infinite Self, and reminded them of their Divine Purpose.

My internal perceptions developed. I could recognize the energy of different Archangels and Divine Beings just by calling their name and watching them come forth into my awareness. I became skilled at internally perceiving blocks and discord in my own or another's energy field, and I could "see" them dismantling as I used the Healing Tools.

Meeting Divine Mother

As my subtle perceptions became more clear, I discovered that I could drop deeper into the Infinite Wholeness and watch the unbounded Unified Field manifest itself into form. It was a beautiful, majestic, Love-filled process.

I frequently had internal visual images of a wave of Light coming out of the unbounded Source and expanding, dividing, and falling back into Source, just like the waves on an ocean rise, expand, and fall back. The feeling of exultation while observing the Light rise, expand, and curl back on itself was tremendous.

One day as I watched, I became curious and sent a question to the wave:

"Who are you?"

Immediately, the wave expanded and rose up as if with arms out wide, and I heard:

"I am the Divine Mother, Mother of Creation. This is how I create!"

I was awed! I studied Her more carefully. She was creating. She was creating the universe. And She was revealing this birth process to me.

The Silent unbounded Source welled up and turned into a wave of Light that expanded and filled my field of vision. Then it divided and expanded more, with drops and rivulets of light splashing off the original wave. They in turn combined and merged with each other to build more advanced stages of creative development, and it went on and on: dividing, expanding, combining, and building more and more complex light forms. It came to me that these were the subtle light forms and flows—vibrational frequencies—that eventually become atoms, molecules, cells, and concrete material objects.

It was a huge display of creative power in action. I was stunned with the majesty of it all. The

Divine Mother was revealing Herself to me. I felt myself internally bowing to the Mother and becoming absorbed in Her. Her beauty and grace were breath-taking. She showed me more. I got the distinct feeling that she enjoyed displaying Her creativity. She wanted me to understand how life manifests.

She demonstrated how She creates from Infinite Silent Pure Being, what physics calls the Unified Field. She moves it into form as sound and light. "Let there be light" is in fact what happens. The Creator rises up as a wave of Light and like a master orchestra conductor, directs Light to build, change, separate, and combine into new forms, new orchestrations. It was spectacular!

Knowledge began coming to me about Her. I was hearing and knowing, "I am One with everything. All aspects of God are Me in different forms. I come forth again and again to bring Myself to you in whatever form you can receive Me."

She was talking to me. I was in Her Home. It was so simple, so natural. I watched Her demonstrate Her creative process. She was moving or "stirring" the un-manifest Wholeness into motion, into form.

It was only later that I realized I was in the place between Pure Being and Manifest Form, the connection, gap or junction between these two opposites. Yet they weren't opposite, they were the same thing, only one was formless and one had form. She wanted me to know that they were really both the same.

I was now meeting Her face to face. I knew She had the answers to every question I could ever ask. I had found what I began seeking a long time ago when I set out to find the Kingdom of Heaven. I had found my way to Her. At last, I was "shaking hands with God."

A Personal Relationship with Divine Mother

Since meeting Divine Mother, I find that I am constantly being pushed more and more deeply into Love. I am being led to open my heart to the biggest possible experience of Love.

Divine Mother keeps opening opportunities for me to uncover more of the experience of union with God. One level of union isn't enough. It has to become a constant awakening to the ever-opening well of the power of Love. When this power of Love is resisted, even unknowingly, tremendous pain results. When this power of Love is allowed, it creates a life of freedom, joy, and access to anything you could ever want to know.

I was looking for a personal relationship with God, and I was given these Tools to help me find it. Now I am sharing these Tools with you so that you can find it too. This personal relationship is the most joyful and practical way to move though life on earth.

I am consistently tuning myself to Divine Mother's Intelligence and using it to solve the problems in my life. My heart is expanding and opening into exalted experiences of Love. Divine Wisdom is showing me how the universe works. Having this knowledge, I can attune myself to the universal flow of life force and use it to enrich and enhance every part of my life here on earth.

I am constantly awed by the intimate connection, the unity I have with all life, and I am learning how to live my life in harmony with all life in creation.

I have become One with Divine Mother. The view of creation from my perspective as Divine

Mother is that all is One immovable presence, and yet I move it within myself with grace and delight, creating awesome, wonderful marvels. There is no fear, only Love and the certainty that everything can be managed with ease. Challenges turn into adventures.

I continue to work with Divine Mother and use her Healing Tools in more and more refined ways. She wants a personal relationship with you too. She can help us move through this challenging time on our planet. She is here now because Her nurturing Love is desperately needed to bring humanity back into balance.

You are deeply loved and very special. Divine Mother invites you into an intimate personal relationship with Her now.

Part Two

Divine Mother's Healing Tools

Chapter 6

Introduction to the Tools

Basic Concepts

It took me years of exploration and experience to develop these Healing Tools. I realized later that they had been gradually revealed to me by Divine Mother. They can empower anyone to significantly improve their life and come into an intimate relationship with Divine Mother. The Tools are powerful. I want to help you to understand them so you can use them most effectively. Here, I have tried to explain as simply as possible some concepts at the basis of these Tools.

Who Is Divine Mother?

People often ask me, "Who is Divine Mother?" Divine Mother is the same as Mother-Father God. The mother aspect of God is coming forth at this time because our world needs Her so desperately. She is here to unite Her human family. We have become lost, isolated, afraid, and conflicted. We need Her qualities of unconditional Love, nurturing, nourishment, tenderness, kindness, and tremendous creativity to move us forward on our path of evolution. Mother God is coming to bring us home.

She is both personal and universal, and wants a relationship with each of us.

If you already have a relationship with God as the Father, you also have a relationship with God as the Mother. They are One.

You Are a Divine Being

My healing work with many people over time has revealed to me the great depth of human suffering on this earth plane. The social and cultural structures, and even many of the religions perpetuate the idea that humans are small, flawed beings, unworthy in the eyes of God. But this is not the Truth.

You are a Divine Being in a physical form. You are Infinite and Whole. It is important to know who you are.

The fear, shame, and unworthiness have obscured the Truth of your Self. You are a Divine

Being who has come to Earth to live in a physical body for the purpose of helping Mother Earth transform.

During your time here on Earth, you have forgotten who you are. The density of the earth plane caused you to forget your infinite status and you identified with the small limitations of life: death, fear, guilt, shame, and unworthiness.

I have discovered that Divine Mother loves us unconditionally. She is here now to elevate us by giving us the experience of who we really are. It is time to embrace our Divine Nature and live as a Divine Being in a physical form.

As you use these Healing Tools, you will be uncovering and discovering the beauty and magnificence of your own Divine Nature. Divine Mother's Healing Tools break you free from the mistaken identity of the small self, and restore your awareness of your Divine Self.

What is the Infinite Wholeness?

Definition

Wholeness is something I talk about a lot in these Healing Tools, and I want you to understand what it is. This book is based upon Wholeness, something that is intangible, invisible, and yet builds everything in the universe. Wholeness is the Infinite Source of everything in Creation, including your life. It could be called the Infinite Presence, the unified field, the quantum ground state, the unmanifest pure potential, or Pure Being. It is everywhere, in everything, in the space between things, yet it is not a form. Your True nature is this formless Wholeness. It is your Self.

The Experience of Wholeness

By practicing Divine Mother's Tools, you are going to experience Wholeness. Her Healing Tools dip you into the Infinite Wholeness as you say the words. At first, you might not notice it. Be patient and use the Tools as instructed, and you will find that your life changes for the better. This is the result of dipping into the Wholeness. As your awareness expands to embrace the Wholeness, you will become aware of it as the constant silent presence of your True Self.

The First Form of Wholeness Is Divine Mother

Divine Mother is both the Infinite Wholeness and the first manifestation of Wholeness when it comes into existence as a form. Divine Mother, as the personal expression of Wholeness, then manifests everything. As a mother gives birth to a child, She gives birth to the universe. All of the beings in the world are the children of Mother God.

The Experience of Divine Mother

By experiencing Divine Mother, you are experiencing Wholeness and a personal form of Wholeness. The Divine Mother Tools in this book use the qualities of Divine Mother to change your experience of life. She is in each of these Tools. When you use the Divine Light Tool, She is the Divine Light that pours into you. She is the Divine Love that saturates you. She is the power behind the Go Command and the Break Command and all the other Healing Tools that clear and lift you. So you're going to be developing an intimate relationship with Divine Mother as you use Her Healing Tools. You will become more and more intimate with Her, until you eventually experience that you and Divine Mother are One.

How These Tools Work

Divine Mother's Healing Tools dissolve the blockages in the flow of your life force, and you become centered and connected to the Divine power that moves you successfully through life.

When the life energy deep within flows through you without obstruction, everything works in your life. You are happy, healthy, productive, and creative. When life force is blocked, life becomes difficult. Problems arise on the surface of life in health, finances, relationships, and other challenges. You can feel stuck, depressed, lost, frustrated, sick, or afraid.

Releasing the blocks on the subtle level changes the effect on the surface level. When these blocks are released from your energy field, you can have better health, fulfilling relationships, and abundance.

These Tools give you the ability to work at the deepest levels, to change any situation, no matter how long-standing. They support the development of powerful competence to manage your life. Divine Mother is putting transformational power into your hands with these Tools.

Using Divine Mother's Healing Tools

Stay in the Heart

Divine Mother resides in your heart. The more you can let your awareness embrace your heart, the more connected you become to Divine Mother. Plan to speak or read these Tools with your heart voice. Stay soft in your heart, and intend to open to Divine Mother. This will enable you to connect with Her. She is the one who is doing the healing. You don't have to feel responsible for it yourself. As you reference Her presence in your heart, you will find the healing becomes much easier and more fluid. She is your guide during this healing process. Any time you feel lost or confused, call upon Her. She is with you every time you use these Healing Tools.

Breathing into your heart or putting your hand on your heart will help you connect to your heart. The healing sequence begins with the Heart Exercise to facilitate this before the Invocation of the Divine Beings. This process will help you stay in your heart.

Notice Your Inner Life

Energy is changing as you use these Tools. What you are saying in each Tool is happening. Contracted energies are expanding and becoming more Light-filled. You can notice these changes.

As you begin to notice what is going on, you will start to have a sense during your daily life when something in you or another person needs to be healed.

A helpful practice when starting to use this healing method is to notice how you feel before you begin to read the Divine Mother Tools, and then notice how you feel after you have read them. Let the noticing be innocent, no judgments, no right or wrong. Just notice. Have you changed? Having this awareness will serve you as you refine your ability to work with these Tools.

Use the Power of Your Voice

In the first weeks of using these Tools, read them out loud. Your voice has power, and as you read Divine Mother's words in these Tools and exercises, the vibration resonates in the surroundings. Sound vibration affects the atmosphere. Speaking the Divine words out loud brings Divine qualities into the environment as well as to you.

However, the more you use Divine Mother's Tools, the more you will find yourself drawn to speak them silently. Your attention settles within, and you gradually focus at deeper inner levels. This occurs spontaneously.

Using Divine Mother's Tools for Others

Divine Mother's Tools are presented in this book for your personal healing. To use the Tools and techniques for another person, your family, a group, or situation, simply change the wording to reflect this. For example, where it says, "Divine Light is pouring into me now," say, "Divine Light is pouring into my family now. Divine Light is filling their energy fields on every level …" For a world concern, say, "Divine Love is pouring into Mother Earth. Mother Earth is receiving Divine Love on every level …" You could also name a specific place or situation in the world. For an individual you can say, "The Wholeness of Divine Grace is completely filling _____ [name] now. He/she is receiving Divine Grace …" This customizes Divine Mother's Tools for specific situations.

People often ask if it's necessary to get permission from someone to do a healing for them. No, it is not necessary. Divine Mother's Tools work from the Unified Field, the deepest level of creation where we are all One. You are healing another from a place of Oneness with them, so essentially you are healing yourself. If you are aware of discord in someone else, the discord is resonating in your system and making you uncomfortable. So heal it, and both of you will benefit. No permission is needed, and you are giving a blessing to that person.

Recommended Sequence for Using the Tools

Divine Mother recommends a specific sequence for using Her Tools. Follow the suggested order to gain maximum benefit. This sequence increases the Divine Energy in your system, while at the same time targeting the release of discordant energy. As the Divine Energy builds, blocks and obstructions in your energy field dissolve.

There are two kinds of Divine Mother Tools: Clearing Tools and Divine Tools. The Clearing Tools directly address and dissolve the blocks in your system. The Divine Tools lift your vibration into the frequency of Divine Mother, uniting you with Her. Most of the Clearing Tools appear towards the beginning of the sequence for immediate relief of the presenting discord. The latter part of the sequence lifts your vibration and strengthens you so that discord can no longer accumulate.

The process is subtle and powerful. For maximum results, use all the Tools in the sequence in one sitting. A full healing session is strongly advised as a daily spiritual practice. When time is limited, there is a short sequence to use, and even a mini-session for quick spiritual cleansing any time.

Specialized Tools

Specialized Divine Mother Healing Tools are included in this book, besides the ones in the suggested sequences. One or more of these tools can be added to any Divine Mother Healing session if you perceive a need. Or you can use them on their own, outside a healing session.

For example, the Self-Love Exercise is very valuable to use on its own on a daily basis. The Flow of Love Exercise is useful when you want to get in touch with Divine Mother. You can transform the energy of any uncomfortable experience by spinning Ascending Light in it.

It is good to become familiar with these Specialized Tools so you can use them when a particular need arises.

Using This Manual

Read through the Healing Tools and their explanations to understand the purpose and power of each Tool. When you want to do a healing, turn to Part Three of this book. There you will find the Tools sorted into the Full Sequence, the Short Sequence, the Mini-Sequence, and Healing on the Run. Take your pick of which session sequence you want to use, and read through it. Each Tool is powerful in itself and can always be used individually apart from the sequence.

Eventually, you will know the Tools so well that you will be able to remember them and use them anywhere, anytime whether you have this manual or not. You will carry with you the power to transform any condition.

Chapter 7

Basic Tools and Explanations

Heart Exercise – Short Form

To start a Divine Mother healing session:

Breathe into the heart center, not just the heart organ, but the whole chest area. Breathe as if the breath is coming through the front of the chest into the heart and soften in the heart to receive the breath. Allow the heart to open, like a flower opening its petals, to receive the warm, soft breath.

If you can't keep your attention in the heart, take many strong, deep breaths (10 to 15) into the chest area. The deep breaths quiet mental activity and then you can focus attention on the heart.

The breath carries life energy. Soften in the heart as your receive the breath. Notice the flow of breath moving into the heart center.

Continue to put your attention on the heart center, which is the whole chest area, not just the heart organ. Notice if there is any tightness or discomfort there. If there is, breathe into it, allowing the breath to move through it, opening it up, and moving the flow of breath through the discomfort.

Practice the Heart Exercise for a minute or two before beginning the Invocation. This dissolves blockages and connects you to your heart. Keep breathing into the heart throughout the Invocation as you unite with Divine Mother and the Great Beings of the universe. Then begin the healing sequence.

Doing the Heart Exercise and then going right into the Invocation helps you connect to Divine Mother, who is actually conducting the healing. This process is designed to move you out of your small self and settle you into your heart.

About the Heart Exercise – Short Form

Note: The Heart Exercise – Short Form is an abbreviated version of the Heart Exercise – Long Form, which is in the Specialized Tools section of this book.

Why Start with the Heart Exercise?

The Heart Exercise – Short Form moves your attention immediately into your heart center, the home of Divine Mother. You are dropping out of your mental energies into your heart because that's where the power is. Your mind is useful, but your real power lies in the intelligence of your heart. Your heart is where you are One with Divine Mother. With your attention there, the power of Divine Mother can move through you to conduct the healing.

Why Use the Breath?

We use the breath because it carries life energy to the body. When focused on the heart, it enlivens the Divine Energy within your heart. At the same time, it releases any energetic blocks from your heart.

Many people have numbed their heart energies, believing that this protects them from being hurt. The breath wakes up the heart so that it can function fully.

What Are You Looking For?

This Tool directs you to notice what's in the heart. It could be anything, whatever comes up for you. It could be a physical sensation, like tightness or pain. It could be emotional, like sadness or fear. It could be an energy, like heaviness, vague discomfort, darkness, or light. It might be more subtle, like space or quiet.

No matter what it is, or how insignificant you may consider it, just intend to breathe into it. This allows the breath to begin healing any blocks or obstructions in your heart. If there are no obstructions, it takes you deep into the heart, centering you in your Divine Self.

What If I Can't Keep My Focus on My Heart?

If your attention keeps moving off the heart and into the head, put your hand on your heart. Feeling the pressure of the hand will help keep your focus on the heart. Then breathe through the back of your hand into your heart, and notice what is there. If all you are feeling is the pressure of the hand on the heart, breathe into that. This will get you started.

Invocation of the Divine Beings

Start by saying:

I am Whole. I am One with God. I am One in the Infinite Wholeness of all that is. I call upon Almighty Mother-Father God and all of the beautiful expressions of Divine Love who know and live the Wholeness of Divine Truth.

I call upon these Great Divine Beings now ...

Here, name those Great Beings who recognize their Wholeness and Oneness with God. Below is a list of some of the Divine Ones the author calls upon. It is not necessary to invite all of them. You may call upon the names below or only those who are familiar to you. Or just call upon Divine Mother or Mother-Father God.

I call upon the presence of Divine Mother in Her many aspects. I call upon Mother Mary (Christian), **Shekhina** (Jewish), **the Divine Presence of Fatima** (Islam), **Mother Lakshmi, Saraswati, Durga, Kali, Parvati** (Hindu). **I invite Tara and Quan Yin** (Buddhist), **Amaterasu** (Shinto), **White Buffalo Calf Woman** (Native American). **I call upon Gaia, Mother Earth, and Prakriti, Mother Nature. I invite all the expressions of Divine Mother from the world's traditions of Truth.**

I invite those Great Beings and Master Teachers around whom many of the world's spiritual traditions have grown. I call upon Jesus Christ and the Holy Spirit (Christian), **Abraham and Moses** [Jewish], **the Divine Presence of Mohammed** (Islam), **Lord Buddha** (Buddhist), **Lao Tzu** (Taoist), **Lord Krishna, Lord Ram, Lord Vishnu, Lord Shiva, Lord Brahma** (Hindu).

I call upon the Archangels: Archangels Michael, Gabriel, Raphael, Uriel, Zadkiel, Chamuel, Jophiel, Metatron, and all Archangels. (You may wish to add others.)

I invite the Ascended Masters: Babaji, Sananda, Serapis Bey, Saint Germain, Brother Francis of Assisi, Lady Nada, and all the Ascended Masters. (You may wish to add others.)

I invite the Gurus (Spiritual Teachers). (Name those fully enlightened Gurus who are significant in your life.)

Continue with:

There is a protective sphere of Holy Light surrounding me now, creating a sacred space. Archangel Michael and his legions of angels guard and protect this sacred space, so that only the energies of the Archangels, Ascended Masters, and Beings of Light holding the Wholeness of Divine Truth may enter this space. Archangel Michael stands in front of me, behind me, to the right of me, to the left of me, above me, and below me. I am safe and protected within this sacred sphere of Holy Light.

The loving, liquid, golden, healing substance of Divine Love is continually pouring into me throughout this healing session, allowing all the healing, lifting, and energy shifting to be smooth, comfortable, and complete.

I invite these Great Divine Beings to be present here now, to lift and heal me.

If there is a specific issue say:

Please heal the issue of _____

Name whatever you want to have healed. If there is not a specific issue at this time, continue with the healing sequence and know that the healing will be for your highest good in all areas.

Thank you Divine Mother, and so it is.

About the Invocation of the Divine Beings

Invocation

You begin with a statement of Divine Truth, acknowledging your Wholeness and Oneness with God. The true basis of all unhappiness in life comes from the belief in separation from God. Divine Mother's Tools and techniques are designed to dissolve this untruth.

You call upon all these Divine Teachers and Masters at the beginning because every Divine name has infinite power. Saying their names activates the energy of those Great Ones and unites you with those who already know they are One with God. The invocation lifts your vibration into this Divine frequency.

Saying the Divine names from all these spiritual traditions of the world with the intention to unify with their Divine Energy, helps to unify our world family.

There are other Divine Beings of the vibration of Divine Truth that are not included on this list. You may certainly invoke them if you know they are consciously aware of their Oneness with the Divine.

If you are unsure whether a teacher or guide you wish to invite has gained the status of conscious Oneness with God say, "I invite the Divine Presence of _____," addressing their Divine Self. Everyone has a Divine Self, even though they may not be consciously operating from it. If you preface the invitation this way, then you are safe, knowing you are staying within the Wholeness of Divine consciousness in your invocation.

Sphere of Protective Light

The sphere of protective Light creates a sacred space within which you can open deeply and heal. It activates a shield of Light around you which protects you from the interference of negative energies. By regularly establishing this sacred space, you will develop a powerful protective shield of Light around you all the time.

The Protection of Archangel Michael

Archangel Michael is the archangel of protection. Calling upon him establishes his presence around you. He guards the sacred space and dissolves any negative energies that might approach. He also guards you as you heal and transform your energy field.

Divine Power Is Conducting the Healing

Don't put effort into this procedure. Calling upon the Divine Beings ensures that they are going to do the work for you. Settle into your heart, then let go, and innocently read the Tools, confident that the Divine Beings are directing the process.

Softening Exercise

This exercise uses the power of attention and intention. The process is to move the attention to a specific place with the intention to soften there.

Softening is a relaxing or letting go of rigid boundaries. You are putting your attention on a specific place and then softening the boundaries of that place, letting your awareness flow beyond the boundaries.

Read the steps of the exercise, practicing it while you read it. Let your attention go to the area of the body named and soften there. The intent to soften is enough; don't try to make it happen.

Go slowly and pause each time you soften.

Here is the process:

> Soften in the heart …
> Soften in the heart center, not just the heart organ, but the whole chest area.
> Move your attention to the throat, soften in the throat …
> Soften the boundaries of the throat.
> Move your attention to the brow, which includes the brow area and the place between the eyebrows, often called the third eye. The attention is on the brow area.
> Soften in the brow/third eye …
> Soften at the top of the head, the crown …
> Soften at the base of the spine in the same way as you have been doing in the other energy centers.
> Soften in the pelvic area, the area below the navel, letting go in the pelvic area.
> Soften in the navel …
> Soften in the solar plexus, the diaphragm area above the navel.
> Soften again in the heart …

Repeat the above sequence at least three more times, ending by softening in the heart. Then continue with the following sequence:

> Soften in the cells.
> Soften in the brain, letting the brain melt like butter on a hot day.
> Soften in the whole body.
> Soften in the space around the body, the auric field.
> Soften in the navel.
> Soften in the heart.

Finish by inwardly saying:

I am Whole and One with All That Is.
Thank you Divine Mother, and so it is.

About the Softening Exercise

What Does the Softening Exercise Do?

The Softening Exercise quiets and balances your system. By softening in each energy center of your body in the order given, you begin to move the flow of life force from center to center creating a stream of life energy that flows up and down your body in a very integrated pattern through these chakra centers. This empowers the chakras and smooths out confused or discordant energies within them, creating health and vitality in your system.

By consistently doing this, you expand the awareness through each point into the Infinite level of life. The Infinite can then create within that chakra.

The combination of focusing your attention and then softening opens the deeper levels of each chakra center to healing. Softening connects you with your Infinite Source. If the body is in need of healing, healing will take place by virtue of the connection to the Infinite Source.

Why Start and End with the Heart?

Beginning with the heart is important. The heart center is the central energy center of the body. The infinite flow of life force in the universe is easy to access through the heart, because the heart is always connected to the Source of the flow. Also, beginning with the heart center helps the other centers easily embrace the flow of this infinite life energy. Beginning at the heart center places you in the home of Divine Mother. Ending at the heart center leaves you in the home of Divine Mother.

A Suggestion for Using the Softening Exercise

Many people who have trouble settling into meditation start with the Softening Exercise and find it helps them easily slip into a very quiet, deep meditation.

Divine Light

Soften in the heart.

Pause for a moment after every sentence, and read slowly. Repeat any of these paragraphs more than once if desired.

> **Divine Light is pouring into me now. Divine Light is filling my energy field on every level. Divine Light is increasing within me now. I am receiving more and more Divine Light, moment by moment. Divine Light is healing every limitation within my energy system and opening me to Wholeness now.**

Pause and continue reading slowly.

> **Divine Light is releasing all discord within my system now and opening me to more Divine Light. Divine Light is flooding my energy system now. I accept Divine Light within me now. I know that Divine Light is increasing its presence within my system and illuminating my entire energy field. The most refined, sublime quality of Light in creation is opening in my energy system and lifting my energy field into resonance with Sacred Light vibration.**

> **Divine Light is healing me now. This Sacred Light is lifting, opening, cleansing, and healing my entire system, and allowing the presence of Light to increase within me now. Divine Light is filling every organ, tissue, cell, atom, and particle of my body. Divine Light continues filling me and healing my entire energy field. I am inundated, saturated, permeated, and penetrated with Divine Light.**

Pause and continue to read slowly.

> **Divine Light is emerging from Source and overflowing on every level of my energy field, nourishing my system with more Divine Light. I am receiving wave after wave of Light. I am filled with Light. More Divine Light is awakening in my entire system and releasing all that is not Whole.**

> **The Wholeness of Divine Light fills me now. All energies of limitation and lack are dissolving as Divine Light vibrates throughout my energy field. I am held in Divine Light. I am bathed in Divine Light. I am healed in Divine Light. I am lifted, opened, cleansed, and freed in Divine Light.**

> **Thank you Divine Mother, and so it is.**

About Divine Light

Why Use Divine Light?

The universe is made of Divine Light. "Let there be Light" is the first intention of the Creator. All spiritual traditions recognize the creative and transformative power of Light.

This Tool creates a Divine situation in your life, awakening your connection to the Creator, who creates with Light all the time. Together with the Creator, you begin to create a Light-filled life. Darkness dissolves, density collapses, fear disappears, pain disperses. These are some of the effects of healing with Light.

Activating Divine Light

Divine Light is present all the time. The Divine Light Tool activates the presence of Divine Light by bringing your attention to it. When you read the Divine Light Tool, everything described in it happens as you say it.

Noticing Divine Light

When you use this Tool, intend to notice the Divine Light. You are learning to perceive with your subtle senses, so be patient if you don't notice Light immediately. There may be a vague feeling or an awareness of Light. You might feel lighter in weight. You might feel your burdens lifting. You might notice liveliness or tingling. The experience of Light is unique to everyone and changes with continued use of the Tool.

You Are Multi-Leveled

You are a multi-leveled being with many layers to your existence. This technique heals every layer. It takes you deeper and deeper into the root level of any problem. Every presenting challenge on the surface experience of life, whether illness, relationships, or money, is caused by discordant energy at a deeper level. With these Tools, you can heal the problems on the surface by attending the root level.

Layering Divine Light

You are layering Divine Light around you and within you with this Tool. By repeating the words many times, you build a strong field of Light around you. This provides a very powerful protective field and dissolves the density in your system.

Customizing the Use of Divine Light

You can fill any person or condition with Divine Light. Simply replace the word *me* with a person's name or name the challenge. For example, "Divine Light is filling my finances now. Divine Light is filling my finances on every level ..." or "Divine Light is filling my mother now ..."

Experiences Using Divine Light

When a friend's daughter was having surgery, she filled the operating room, the doctor, and all the attendants with Divine Light before and during the surgery. The surgery went well, and she was at peace through the whole process.

A man was having financial problems. He consistently filled his finances, checkbook, investments, and bank account with Divine Light. The problems were resolved.

An accountant had a business meeting she knew would be difficult, so she poured Divine Light into the meeting and all the people there. She reported that the conference was smooth and productive.

Closing Holes in Your Aura

I call upon Divine Mother and Archangel Michael to close all doors, openings, holes, portals, and pathways anywhere in my multi-leveled energy system to all limited (*those that limit your Wholeness*) **planes, domains, dimensions, spheres, realms, and locations anywhere in creation.**

I command in the name of Divine Mother that all doors, openings, holes, portals, and pathways anywhere in my multi-leveled energy system are now closed and sealed to the following levels:

Go through the list one at a time and after naming each limited level say, **"Close!"** and see doors slam throughout all levels of your energy field. Then see, know, or feel the doors are closed and sealed.

> **I close doors to the astral plane ... CLOSE!** (Includes disembodied earthbound spirits)
> **I close doors to the limited extra-terrestrial entities ... CLOSE!**
> **I close doors to the inter-dimensional entities ... CLOSE!** (Other subtle life forms)
> **I close doors to false gods ... CLOSE!** (Anything you make more powerful than your Infinite Self)
> **I close doors to lost souls ... CLOSE!** (Beings who have lost their evolutionary path)
> **I close doors to negative thought forms ... CLOSE!**
> **I close doors to all dense, low-frequency beings ... CLOSE!**
> **I close doors to the fear and negativity in the world consciousness ... CLOSE!**
> **I close doors to all unknown limited beings ... CLOSE!**

Repeat from the authority of your Divine Self:

> **These doors, openings, holes, portals, and pathways are now closed and sealed, in the name and through the power of Divine Mother, in the name and through the power of Archangel Michael.**

Again, image doors closing and sealing all around you. Focused attention on the holes closing is important.

Then say:

> **Any energetic configurations or attracting mechanisms around these now closed holes and openings are dismantled, broken, dissolved, and released.**

**I am now opening into my authentic Self and moving through my individual
life with Grace, Power, and Divine Integrity.**

See or feel or know that a strong shield of protective Light is all around you, very vibrant and
powerful.

End by saying:

**I am aligned with Truth. I am Whole.
Thank you Divine Mother, and so it is.**

About Closing Holes in Your Aura

What Is the Aura?

The aura is a field of energy around your physical body. A strong aura is like a strong shield
around the body, protecting it and allowing you to function comfortably in the world. The
energy that composes your aura interacts with other energy fields in this complex creation. Often
disruptive energies in the environment interact with your aura and compromise you.

What Are Holes in Your Aura?

"Holes" in your aura are openings in the energy around the body that allow energies from
outside to pass into your energy field. Throughout your life, these holes or openings may have let
in a lot of the fear, pain, and anger of the world, and all of it would have had an effect on you,
even weakened you.

By closing the holes and openings in your aura to negativity, you become much stronger,
clearer, and more stable. It is important to maintain a strong auric field. The negativity and stress
of others bounces off or is dissolved by a strong auric field and cannot impact you adversely.
Yet, positive energies can flow into you, while your gifts and creativity can flow out into the
environment.

Why Is It Important to Close Holes in the Aura?

Closing holes in your aura allows you to stay in touch with your Highest Self. You are a Divine
Being in a physical form. You are growing to recognize that you are Infinite. You are rising to
the highest level of life in union with God. Lower vibrations do not serve your highest good, so
you are closing your aura to these lower vibrational influences. You are closing your auric field
to the planes in creation that contract you into a small, fearful self instead of expanding you into
recognizing your True Infinite Self.

Why Do We Get Holes in the Aura?

You get holes in your aura when you are no longer acting, thinking, and being in your Highest Self. Some things that open your aura are: negative thinking, giving up your power to others, or compromising your principles to accommodate others. Physical illness can also open the aura because the system becomes weak and incapable of maintaining a strong vibrational field. Alcohol, cigarettes, and drugs can also open the aura, because they destabilize the vibrational system.

When Should I Close My Aura?

We recommend that you close holes in your aura every day. Do it first thing in the morning and just before going to bed at night. Other times to close your aura are when people around you are negative or angry. This Tool closes your energy to their anger, fear, guilt trips, attacks, complaints, coercion, or manipulation. You are not closing to their True Self; you are closing to the limitations fueling their negativity.

Suggestions for Using Closing Holes in Your Aura

When anyone starts to unload their negativity on you, immediately close your aura to their agitated energies.

After meditating, you may be ultra-sensitive to environmental negativity. To help maintain your inner peace, close your aura to the outer discord.

In a public place like a mall or a store, if you feel spacey or over-stimulated, close your aura to feel more comfortable and clear.

When you feel that someone is trying to manipulate you by making you feel guilty or afraid, close your aura to them and make your own decisions.

First Go Command

This Tool clears the discord and blockages that have accumulated in the subtle fields of your energy system and are compromising the full expression of your True Self. Later in the healing session, the Deep Go Command Tool will clear blockages at even deeper levels.

Breathe into the heart. Say:

> **I call upon Divine Mother and all the Divine Beings to release and clear all discordant energies, blockages, and confusion from the following levels of my system.**

First, clear the <u>emotional level</u>.

Say lovingly but firmly from your Divine Authority, not from your small self:

> **I now address all blockages and discord at the emotional level of my energy field. Go into the Light. Go … Go … Go … Go into the Light …**

As needed, repeat:

> **Go into the Light. Go … Go … Go … Go into the Light … Go … Go … Go … Go into the Light. In the name of God, I command you to go into the Light now.**

Continue repeating **"Go"** until you notice a shift, like a sense of expansion, a deep breath, or a settling indicating there has been a release.

You are clearing layers of your emotional system. By repeating **"Go into the Light"** over and over, you clear deeper and deeper layers. Keep repeating **"Go"** until you feel clear and complete at each level.

As you proceed, alternate saying **"Go"** with filling the level with Diving Light. Say:

> **Divine Light is filling the emotional level, Divine Light is pouring into the emotional level, Divine Light is saturating the emotional level, more and more Divine Light fills the emotional level.**

Then return to saying **"Go, Go into the Light …"** until you sense that level is clear and complete.

Next, clear the <u>mental level</u>. Say:

I now address all blockages and discord at the mental level of my energy field. Go into the Light. Go, Go, Go …

At every level, follow the same instructions for clearing as stated above.

Now clear the <u>etheric level</u>. Say:

I now address all blockages and discord at the etheric level of my energy field. Go into the Light. Go, Go, Go …

Follow instructions as stated above.

Clear the <u>physical level</u>. Say:

I now address all blockages and discord at the physical level of my energy field. Go into the Light. Go, Go, Go …

Follow instructions as stated above.

Clear the <u>astral level</u>. Say:

I now address all blockages and discord at the astral level of my energy field Go into the Light. Go, Go, Go …

Follow instructions as stated above.

Clear the <u>causal level</u>. Say:

I now address all blockages and discord at the causal level of my energy field. Go into the Light. Go, Go, Go …

Follow instructions as stated above.

Clear the <u>celestial level</u>. Say:

I now address all blockages and discord at the celestial level of my energy field. Go into the Light. Go, Go, Go …

Follow instructions as stated above.

Clear the level of <u>Pure Spirit</u>. Pure Spirit is always clear. Here, we clear any mental, emotional, and spiritual misconceptions which limit the experience of this level. Say:

I now address all blockages and discord at the level of Pure Spirit. Go into the Light. Go, Go, Go …

Follow instructions as stated above.

Finally, clear the <u>Avenue of Awareness</u>, which governs the way life is perceived. Say:

I now address all blockages and discord in the Avenue of Awareness. Go into the Light. Go, Go, Go …

Follow instructions as stated above.

Then conclude by saying:

All limited energies, entities, and negative programs are now released and let go on every level of my energy system. All doors, openings, holes, portals, or pathways to these areas are now closed and sealed.

See, know, and feel your aura is strong and powerful.

Then say:

I am now opening into the Wholeness of my Authentic Self, and it is flowing through my individual life with Grace, Power, and Divine Integrity.

Thank you Divine Mother, and so it is.

About the First Go Command

Purpose of the First Go Command

There are two Go Commands in the Divine Mother system of Healing Tools. This First Go Command focuses on clearing and healing your energy field of blockages in the various subtle fields making up your system.

We clear the discord in these areas so that deeper issues can be revealed. As these levels of your system clear and come into balance, the connection to your authentic Self is strengthened. From this foundation, continue the recommended sequence of Divine Mother's Healing Tools to release even deeper issues. These deeper issues will be addressed by the Deep Go Command later in the session.

What Is Being Cleared?

We clear the blocks in the flow of your life force. This includes limited energies, entities, negative programs, error belief systems, false identities, fear, shame, unworthiness, and anything else that masks the Truth of who you are. As these release and the flow of your life force is strengthened, your True Divine Nature is revealed, and you move through your individual life with Grace, Power, and Divine Integrity.

Using the Word "Go"

The command "Go" has an impact on the energies that block the flow of your life force. The sound vibration of the word and the Divine authority with which it is spoken dissolve the blockages. Everything in the universe is intelligent and understands "Go into the Light." The command is loving, yet firm. You are sending the energy to its next perfect place to grow and evolve.

Why Repeat "Go" Over and Over?

We are clearing subtle levels of your complex energy system. There are layers within each level. Every "Go" is addressing a deeper layer. You repeat "Go" many times to clear many layers at each level.

You will know that each level is clear when you have a sense of lightness, expansion, or more depth. This sense continues to develop with consistent use of the Tools.

Why Use Divine Light at Each Level?

Divine Light clears discord, lifts vibration, and fills each level with Light. Filling each level with Light clears the discord quickly and efficiently. It also empowers each level to resist additional discord in the system.

Levels of Your Energy Field

Every human has each of these levels in their subtle energy structure:

Emotional – This vibrational field holds the emotions. This Tool dissolves blocks in the emotional field caused by fear. All negative emotions are a form of fear. These fear-based blocks contract your system and you feel pain, shame, anger, or unworthiness. When the emotional field is free from blocks, it becomes healthy and supports positive emotional responses, like happiness, joy, love, and contentment.

Mental – This is the field of thought. This Tool dispels thoughts, belief systems, patterning, and conditioning that do not support the Divine Truth. The Truth is that you are Whole and One with God. The mental level is cleared of thoughts, concepts, and belief systems that make you feel afraid, small, weak, and isolated. What's left are thoughts that let you feel creative, expansive, and Whole.

Etheric – This is an energy field surrounding and permeating the body that feeds the physical body with vital energy necessary for its health and survival. It is impacted by the tension, fear, and pain in the mental, physical, and emotional fields, as well as in your environment. Your use of the Go Command frees the blocks that have been lodged here so that this energy field can fully support your health and vitality.

Physical – This level comprises the physical body. Using this Tool, you dissolve subtle discordant energy in the cells, organs, bones, tissues, chemistry, systems, and everything included in the material physical body.

Astral – This is one of the fields through which human individuality accesses other planes of existence. You have access to a larger astral plane through your individual astral field. This Tool heals limited, disruptive energies, entities, and thought forms that have attached to your individual astral field. This includes all the limited energies we close our aura to when we use the Closing Holes Tool. They inhibit the expression of the Truth of who you are and impede your evolutionary path.

Causal – This is the level where the cause or purpose for your life steers you forward into higher expressions of your Divine Nature. The causal level of a person's system can become blocked with old energies resulting from constricting responses to past life events. If you responded to some life experience with fear, anger, guilt, or any negative, contracting reaction, the energy of that response gets stuck in your system as a loop or blockage in your life energy. The stuck energy causes you to respond again and again in the same old pattern. In this First Go Command, we are releasing that blockage so that your life energy can flow fluidly and powerfully. You are then free to respond differently from an expanded sense of Self.

Celestial – Our individual celestial field enables us to experience the celestial realm. Beings with very high consciousness inhabit this level. We clear this level in ourselves because even in the celestial realm some ego-sense can be present in us or in an unenlightened celestial being, inducing us to attach ourselves to a life that is less than the Supreme experience of Pure Unbounded Self. Because we are focusing on gaining and living our Infinite Self, any ego taint influencing us, even at this level, must be removed.

Pure Spirit – This refers to our Infinite Wholeness, Pure Being, your Divine Self. Pure Spirit is always clear. You are not clearing your Pure Spirit, you are purifying your perception of Pure Spirit. Many times people identify Pure Spirit with an emotion or a mental concept of God. Pure Spirit is beyond mental concepts and definitions. Dissolving these false concepts about God allows the innocent pure experience of the Infinite, Eternal Presence of God.

Avenue of Awareness – This is not one of the levels of the human energy field, but it is important that we clear it. It has to do with your perception of the world around you. As your consciousness grows, the five senses become refined until they perceive the unity of life. Clearing the Avenue of Awareness of blocks assists in developing this perception.

The Avenue of Awareness is the pathway through which our awareness flows. When it is blocked, life appears separate, disconnected, chaotic, and fearful. When the avenue is clear, life is perceived as unified, harmonious, balanced, and Whole.

When the avenue is clear, you are working with the world, not fighting against it. For example, if you hear about a shooting and you put a wall up to disconnect you from that situation, you are separating yourself from the world. If you hear about the shooting and you feel compassion and think, "This is something I need to heal," you stay connected to the world. So when the avenue is clear, a person feels connected. When the avenue is not clear, a person has separated from the world.

During each healing, the experience of the unity of all life is enhanced. As one continues to heal and gain full awakening, one sustains this perception longer and longer. Eventually life is always perceived as unified, harmonious, balanced, and Whole.

Suggestions for Using the First Go Command

Clear all levels of your system as a daily, energetic hygiene. Then you can maintain the power of your True Self expressing in all you do.

Say "Go into the Light" whenever you engage in negative thinking. This is especially helpful with self-critical thoughts. After commanding the thought to go, focus on thoughts of self-respect and self-value.

As a regular routine, use the First Go Command to clear your family or roommates of any limiting energies they have picked up. It will keep your home life joyful and positive.

If you are in a public place and see people speaking harshly to their companions or children, start silently repeating the Go Command to clear the energies constricting their hearts. Then fill them with Divine Love.

When you feel extreme negativity within yourself, use the First Go Command, along with the Break Command, to release the negative energy that is stuck in your system.

Releasing Agreements

Breathe into the heart.

I call upon Divine Mother and Archangel Michael to cancel, release, and dissolve all contracts, agreements, vows, commitments, trades, or exchanges that I may have made in this lifetime or any other that are blocking or limiting my recognition and full expression of who I am now.

These contracts, agreements, vows, commitments, trades, and exchanges are now canceled, released, dissolved, let go, and made null and void, in the name and through the power of Divine Mother, in the name and through the power of Archangel Michael.

Image or "feel" the dissolution of the agreements, or "see" the contract breaking.

All frameworks, structures, circuitry, and grids that have developed as a result of these now canceled contracts and conditions are dissolved, collapsed, broken, released, and let go on every level of my energy field.

Image the frameworks, etc., breaking or dissolving as you say:

Break, Break, Break …

Continue to repeat **"Break,"** energetically breaking the contracts and agreements until the energy is light and free. This can take several minutes.

These frameworks and structures are now completely dissolved, and I am free.

End by saying:

I am filled with Divine Love.
I am aligned with Divine Truth.
I am Whole.
Thank you Divine Mother, and so it is.

About Releasing Agreements

At times in your past, you may have made agreements that no longer serve your highest good. It's important to understand that you are always growing and evolving. Though the agreement may have been valid at the time, agreements made in the past may not serve the level of consciousness and the evolutionary needs you now have.

Why Do We Release Agreements?

Old vows, contracts, and agreements made in different life situations can often prevent the full enjoyment of your life in the present. Many of these may still linger unconsciously in your vibrational system. Some of these agreements may even have been made in previous lifetimes. These contracts need to be released.

The purpose of this Healing Tool is to release past agreements still held in your energy field that do not fully support your present situation.

Most agreements of the past were made when you believed that you were a limited being. You are now accepting the Truth that you are Infinite and Whole. So if agreements made in the past reflect a small self-identity and bind you to a small self-concept, they need to be canceled and released. This Tool sets you free to be your True Self and participate fully in your purpose for this life now.

Suggestions for Using Releasing Agreements

If you feel that vows of poverty, chastity, or self-denial made in a former lifetime are influencing your present life, use this Divine Mother Tool to break those former vows so that you can fully engage in your present life.

Sometimes people make an agreement with themselves to adopt a particular personality to get ahead in life in some way. This eventually creates strain. You may use this Tool to break out of this false façade and begin to relax into being yourself.

If you have been through a divorce and feel that you are having trouble committing to a new relationship, use this Tool to help you let go of the vow you made to your former spouse and free you to be happy in a new relationship.

As a child, you may have made an agreement with yourself to suppress your thoughts and feelings and not reveal all of who you are for fear of exposing yourself to criticism and put-downs. This Divine Mother Tool will help free you from that internal agreement so you can let down your walls and not be afraid to be the real you.

Calling Back Parts

Breathe into the heart.

Say inwardly or out loud:

> **In the name of Divine Mother, I call back all parts of myself that have been separated, isolated, lost, given away, taken, or forgotten. I call these parts back into the Wholeness of my heart now.**

Breathe into the heart center as if the breath is pulling all parts and pieces of yourself back into the Wholeness of your heart.

This may be repeated until you feel you are completely back.

Next say:

> **I call back all parts of myself that have been left behind in former jobs, challenges, people, activities, projects, and relationships. I call these parts back into the Wholeness of my heart.**

Breathe into the heart center as if the breath is pulling all parts and pieces of yourself back into the Wholeness of your heart.

Next say:

> **I call back all my power that I have given away. I call back all the parts of myself that I have hidden.**

Breathe into the heart center as if the breath is pulling all parts and pieces of yourself back into the Wholeness of your heart.

Repeat inwardly or out loud:

> **I call back these parts of myself into the Wholeness of my heart and I claim my Wholeness now.**

Breathe again into the heart, pulling yourself back into the Wholeness of your heart.

Optional:

> You can call yourself back from specific issues as needed.

I call myself back from _____ [name the specific issue].

Examples: **I draw myself back from my relationship with** _____ [name], **my** _____ [family member], **my job at** _____, **the abuse from** _____ [name].

Then repeat:

> **I call back all parts of myself into the Wholeness of my heart and I claim my Whole Self now.**

Any of these may be repeated several times if they are particularly relevant to your life experience.

End with:

> **I welcome all parts of myself back into the Wholeness of my heart now.**
> **I know that I am Whole and One with All That Is.**
> **Thank you Divine Mother, and so it is.**

About Calling Back Parts

Why Call Yourself Back?

Many have had parts of themselves given away, taken away, lost or suppressed. This Tool calls all these fragmented parts back to you.

People often energetically lose parts of themselves in relationships with individuals or groups. This happens when we unknowingly give over our self-authority to another. Then our sense of well-being and self-worth is dependent upon the approval of someone other than our True Self. This Divine Mother Tool brings you back into your True Self, centered in your heart. This is where you need to stay for you to have the most success in a relationship, job, or project. Then you are operating from the Wholeness of your Divine Self and not some small self-concept that depends on someone or something outside of you to justify your value.

Why Use the Breath?

The breath draws life force into you. You are a flow of life energy. If you have given up some part of yourself, you have less life energy.

When you draw yourself back with the breath, you pull life energy into your heart. The breath then opens your heart to receive the parts that had been fragmented. The breath awakens your heart to engage again with the lost pieces and awakens the lost pieces to fill the heart.

Suggestions for Calling Back Parts

Many people give up parts of themselves to their significant others. This Tool enables you to call parts of yourself back that have been given away in the relationship, thus deepening your self-esteem and honest communication.

Those who were abused as children can use this Tool to call themselves back from the situation and from their abuser. Calling yourself back again and again can help you come to terms with the extent to which you may still feel controlled by that person. Much personal power is lost in an abusive situation. This Tool can help you to feel strong and empowered.

It's recommended to call yourself back from any person or group that has coerced or controlled you, either in the past or in the present.

Use this Tool to call yourself back from a parent or relative who was a very strong influence in your life. In this way, you can free yourself from the need for their approval.

Sometimes a relationship doesn't work out, even though you feel deep love for the person. If you still feel invested in a relationship that is over and can't be fully engaged in your present relationship, use this Tool to call yourself back from the former relationship. Then you can fully commit to the new one.

Deep Go Command

After clearing the levels of your energy field earlier in the sequence with the First Go Command, deeper blocks and discord that were previously hidden are often revealed. As you move through the healing sequence, the Deep Go Command is now enlisted.

Breathe into the heart as you read the Tool. Speak from your Divine Self, not your small ego, using the power of your Divine Self to send these constricting energies into the Light.

> **I am Whole and One with All That Is. I am aligned with Divine Truth. In the name of Truth, in the name of Love, I call upon Divine Mother to release all limited energies, entities, and negative programs from my system now.**
>
> **I say to these limitations and blockages:**
>
> **"You must go. Divine Mother is here to take you into the Light. Look for the Light. Look for Divine Mother. Go into the Light and the Love and the Heart of Divine Mother."**

Take two or three more breaths into your heart and say to the blockages:

> **Go into the Light!**

Continue taking deep breaths into the heart and say the word **"Go!"** out loud. Repeat the command:

> **Go into the Light!**

Remember to say this out loud, lovingly but firmly from your Divine Authority, not from your small self.

Optional: To strengthen the command, follow the word **"Go"** by blowing out the breath, as if blowing the limitations away.

Repeat:

> **Go into the Light ... Go ... Go ... Go ... Go into the Light ... Go ... Go ... Go ... Go into the Light ... In the name of God, I command you to go into the Light now. Go ... Go ...**

Optional: Alternate statements to use at your discretion during the process.

I am Infinite and Whole. I command you in the name of my Infinite Self to leave my energy system now. Go into the Light.

I give you permission to go into the Light. Go …

I give myself permission to let go.

As your voice settles and becomes more quiet, continue repeating **"Go into the Light"** inwardly to clear the limited energies at the more subtle levels of your system. Keep softening and know that the healing is being done by Divine Mother, not your individuality.

Keep repeating **"Go"** until you feel centered, expansive, light, and clear. This can take a few minutes or longer, until you feel complete. Then conclude by saying:

I am Whole. I am aligned with Truth.
Thank you Divine Mother, and so it is.

About the Deep Go Command

What Are We Clearing in the Deep Go Command?

In the Deep Go Command, just as in the First Go Command, you, in your Divine Self, tell limiting energies to leave your life stream. The First Go Command cleared your energy field of many intrusive discordant energies. Now, with the Deep Go command you address deeper blockages that have been hidden in your system. Because the surface levels are now clear, you can dive deeper within to release core issues, such as old fears, numbness, depression, trauma, and subconscious belief systems from this lifetime or any other.

The energies we clear in the Deep Go Command are the fundamental obstructions between you and your ultimate union with God. It enables you to experience the Truth of who you are by removing the blocks that hide the Real You.

When to Use This Command

Use it whenever you feel unhappy, angry, frustrated, burdened, overwhelmed, afraid, depressed, or any other negative state. Our society accepts these states as being normal. They are not. They indicate that you have lost your connection to your Divine Self. To be centered and clear in your True Self, these energies, entities, and negative thoughts and emotions must be released.

Command from Your God Self

Say the word "Go" from your God Self, not the small ego. The ego is limited and you will become strained and exhausted if the command comes from the small self. This requires a Divine Command. The God Self is all-powerful and has infinite energy to do the job of clearing.

Using the Word "Go"

The command "Go" has an impact on the energies that obstruct the flow of life force in your energy field. The sound of the word and the Divine authority with which it is spoken dissolve the blockages until your Divine Self is completely unveiled.

The Divine Command "Go into the Light" tells the energy where to go to be lifted and freed. Everything in the universe is intelligent. There are varying degrees of intelligence, but everything has intelligence and understands "Go into the Light." The command is loving, yet firm. You are sending the limited energy to its next perfect place to grow and evolve.

Why Repeat "Go" Over and Over?

Every "Go" is addressing a deeper layer of your energy field, so you repeat "Go" many times to clear many layers of the presenting issue.

Some deep issues may require more than one healing session. You will know that each issue is cleared, for that session, when you have a sense of lightness, expansion, and more depth. This sense develops more with continued use of the Tools.

Can This Command Be Used at Other Times?

Use this Go Command at any time during the healing sequence as other issues come up for healing. You can also use it in daily life when you feel burdened by discordant energies.

To prevent negative energies from entering your system, remember that every negative thought attracts similar thoughts from the environment. These limited, negative vibrations obscure your Infinite Self and make you feel bad. You can command the negative thoughts to "Go into the Light" the instant you notice them throughout your day.

Suggestions for Using the Deep Go Command

Use the Deep Go Command when someone around you is angry, frustrated, harsh, or fearful. Silently repeat the refrain "Go into the Light and the Love and the Heart of Divine Mother" until the person changes. Then fill them with Divine Light.

When you are gripped by a deep depression or are feeling stuck, use the power of the Deep Go Command to blast the stuck energies. Say "Go into the Light" many times as if a wrecking ball or a jack hammer is breaking through the density with each "Go."

If the pain of a past experience comes up to trouble you, start saying "Go into the Light" and soften consistently until you are free of it.

Whenever you feel that a thought, idea, or subtle energy from an outside source is trying to influence you, say "Go into the Light" again and again, until it is gone.

To clear a house or other building of uncomfortable energies, use the Deep Go Command until the atmosphere is clear and light. Then pour in Divine Light.

Break Command

Breathe into the heart and center in your Divine Self, which is in the heart. Continue breathing into the heart and say the following words:

> **I call upon Divine Mother, Archangel Michael, and all the Divine Beings to break, shatter, and dissolve all old patterns, grids, frameworks, structures, and multidimensional matrices that are limiting me or holding negative energies in my system. These structures are now broken, shattered, cracked up, dissolved, released, and completely let go throughout my multidimensional energy system.**

Then take some deep breaths through the heart and chest to activate the life force for healing and transforming your system.

Say the word **"Break!"** out loud (silently if other people not involved in the healing are nearby) and image these structures breaking, shattering, and dissolving. Your imaging tells the energy what to do.

Repeat the word "**Break**!" lovingly but firmly from your Divine Authority, not from your small self.

Say **"Break! Break! Break …"** many times as deeper layers of your system are cleared of the old structures, while continuously imaging the structures breaking and collapsing.

As you say **"Break,"** your voice may soften as you reach the deeper levels of your system. At some point, it will be appropriate to say **"Break"** inwardly. Keep repeating **"Break,"** imaging and feeling the structures dismantling at deeper, more subtle levels. Soften and let go as you break these structures.

In addition to saying **"Break, Break,"** you can use the words, **"Shatter," "Burst," "Smash," "Dissolve," "Melt," "Collapse,"** or other words commanding the dissolution of the old stuck vibrational patterns and structures.

Remember to keep softening and letting go, knowing that the Divine power is doing the breaking, not your individual will.

Notice your energy as you do this and continue until you have a sense of new freedom and expansion in your energy field.

End with:

These old grids, frameworks, and structures are now completely broken, shattered, and dissolved and I am Whole. I am aligned with Truth.

Thank you Divine Mother, and so it is.

Finish by bringing in the Divine Nectar, the liquid Love, to nourish your system and fill the space, now that these grids of untruth are gone. It is the next Tool in the sequence.

About the Break Command

After clearing with the Go Command, now you collapse the vibrational structures that had supported the negative energies in your system. Like the Go Command, speak the Break Command from your Divine Authority, shattering the structures that have compromised you.

What Are We Breaking?

Every thought is a flow of energy. Thoughts about yourself as limited, weak, afraid, unworthy, or ashamed, create an energy contraction in your life force. Life force wants to expand you into greater growth. Thinking any negative thought again and again creates a limiting belief structure, and you become the expression of that belief in the way you live. Whatever your thought patterns created, your thought commands can dismantle.

You are breaking up those thought patterns and belief systems that bind you. The Break Command sets your energy free to embrace the Truth that you are an Infinite Being of Light. You are full of creativity and knowledge that you cannot access when caught in vibrational patterns of fear, shame, and pain. These patterns can cause codependent behaviors, conditioned responses, addictions, depression, and other habits that imprison you and diminish your life force. With this Tool, you can break out of these vibrational cages.

Even the physical body reflects these confining vibrational patterns by eventually compromising your physical system. This may take the form of illness, depression, and other mild to severe discomforts. The Break Command heals all levels of your energy field, including the physical body as you, in your Divine Authority, command the restrictive vibrational patterns to break.

How to Say the Break Command

As in all of Divine Mother's Healing Tools, speak this command from your Divine Self. Don't say the command in the anger or frustration of your small self, but rather in the firm, confident authority of your Divine Self.

Continue softening as you repeat the Break Command. Softening helps you access the deeper layers of the energy.

Image the Structures Breaking

As you speak the command, visualizing structures, frameworks, and grids breaking further communicates to the energy what you want it to do. This imaging is an important aspect of the Break Command.

Why Bring in the Nectar of Love at the End?

It's important to fill the space just healed with positive energy, so that other negative energies don't come in to occupy it. Divine Nectar is a powerful healing substance and acts like a rejuvenating massage oil for the energy system, healing, relaxing, and soothing everything that has been compromised by these structures. Divine Nectar is the flow of Love as a tangible substance and brings your entire system into a deeper level of health and well-being.

Suggestions for Using the Break Command

Use the Break Command if a loved one seems to be stuck in an old pattern of anger and depression, perhaps complaining of things that happened years ago. This Tool will dissolve the energy of a thinking pattern that keeps repeating.

If you have a health issue, use this Tool to break the vibrational structures of the illness in that organ or system. Then intend to fill the area with Divine Love and Divine Light. This helps healing energy flow into the area.

If people, especially family members, start arguing around you, silently repeat "Break, break …" with the intent to break the pattern that traps them in an exchange of negative energy.

Use this Tool to break the energy around long-standing issues like anger, fear, or shame that you have had difficulty letting go of. Dissolving the energy of such issues will make a big difference and help you make positive changes in your life.

Divine Nectar

Breathe into the heart. Soften and let go of any tension. Allow the heart to expand.

Say:

> I am One in the Wholeness of all that is. I am receiving the Love of Divine Mother soaking into me as a nectar-like substance, the pure essence of Divine Love.
>
> I am filling with Divine Nectar now. This Divine Nectar, the essence of Divine Love, is healing me. I am receiving this Liquid Love on every level of my entire energy field. Divine Nectar is pouring into me. I am bathed in Divine Nectar. I am filled with Divine Nectar. I am healed by Divine Nectar.
>
> Liquid Love is healing me as it flows through my system. I am soaking in the sacred Nectar. My heart is being soothed by Liquid Love. The loving flow of Divine Nectar is filling my body, healing every cell, every organ, and every system. My head is filling with Divine Nectar, calming my thoughts, soothing my brain, soaking into my cells. I am filled with Liquid Love.

(Pause and notice the Divine Nectar. Stay soft and centered in the Divine Self in your heart while saying these words.)

> I am letting go of harmful thoughts. I am healing my thinking process. I am opening to Divine Nectar in my head and in my heart. The Nectar is continuing to flood my body. I am healing in this essence of Divine Mother's Love. Divine Nectar is filling me with Liquid Love, and my system is healing the sadness, pain, and suffering.
>
> I am allowing Divine Nectar to increase within me now. I am filling with this Nectar of Love. I am releasing all fear and trusting Divine Nectar to heal everything that is afraid. The waves of Liquid Love are flowing into me, saturating me with their loving caress. I am receiving Divine Nectar.
>
> I open to the flowing Nectar and allow its waves of Love to fill my heart, my body, my mind, and my energy field. I accept Divine Nectar within me now.

Repeat this as often as desired to enrich your system with the healing, soothing presence of Divine Nectar.

> **Thank you Divine Mother, and so it is.**

About Divine Nectar

Divine Nectar fills and soothes you, creating a beautiful environment of healing within. Divine Nectar is the healing balm of the universe.

What Is Divine Nectar?

Divine Nectar is the essence of Divine Love in material form. Divine Nectar can subtly transform the physical body. It comes from the flow of Divine Love in your system as you unite with Divine Mother. As Divine Love penetrates into the physical level, it becomes a nectar-like substance that the physical body can receive. Then Divine Nectar flows through your physical system like a transfusion, delivering its subtle nourishment to the cells.

Why Do We Use It?

The physical body is capable of functioning in a more efficient manner than it is now. Divine Nectar awakens the power of the cells for even greater creativity in the body, helping the body heal and become resistant to disease.

The body is able to heal itself when given the proper support. Divine Nectar heals, relaxes, and soothes everything that has been disrupted by the presence of untruth. It provides powerful subtle support for physical and vibrational healing. It allows the warmth of Liquid Love to melt into you like golden butter on a warm summer day. This Nectar allows your system to relax into the Infinite Source and receive its Divine gifts.

When Do We Use It?

Whenever the body lets go of discordant energies, as it does when you use the Go and Break Commands, it's important to fill it with Divine Nectar. When a vacuum is created due to the release of discord, fill it with Divine Nectar. Then the soothing and healing qualities of the Nectar will support the full recovery of the area that had been compromised.

Use it whenever the body is ill to assist healing. It soothes the system and supports good health.

Suggestions for Using Divine Nectar

Whenever you feel sick, use the Divine Nectar Tool to help heal your body. It allows deep vibrational healing and supports your body's recovery.

Around children or toddlers, read the words of the Divine Nectar Tool out loud. Children will have a sense of the subtle positive energy, and it will produce a positive effect for them.

If you have had surgery, pour in the Divine Nectar often to assist in strengthening the affected area and facilitating recovery.

Whenever you experience roughness because of a sudden change in your life or an emotional upset in your family, bring in the Divine Nectar to smooth and calm the situation.

Divine Love

Soften in the heart.

Pause for a moment after every sentence, and read slowly. Repeat any of these paragraphs more than once if desired.

Divine Love is pouring into me now. I am receiving Divine Love on every level of my existence. I am opening to allow Divine Love to fill me and overflow in my life now.

I accept Divine Love within me now. I am inundated, saturated, permeated, and penetrated with Divine Love. Divine Love fills me again and again on deeper and deeper levels of my existence.

Have a gentle awareness of Divine Love.

Read slowly and pause between each sentence.

I am healing in Divine Love. The Love of Divine Mother is pouring into every atom, cell, organ, and system of my entire physical body. I am flooded with Divine Love, bathed in Divine Love, cleansed by Divine Love.

I open and accept Divine Love within me now on every level of my life expression.

The lively, dynamic energy of Divine Love is cleansing, dissolving, and transmuting all energies of lack and limitation within my energy system. I am opening to the presence of more and more life energy of Divine Love. The vital life energy of Divine Love is transmuting all energies of discord within me now. Radiant, vibrant Divine Love is erasing all error conditioning, all error patterning, all limited belief systems, and all limiting self-concepts.

Divine Love is opening in the deepest areas of my energy field. The oldest, most lost, forgotten, ignored areas of my system are receiving Divine Love. Divine Love is welling up from deep within, dissolving all blocked energy within my energy field. More and more Divine Love is opening within me now. Old ancestral patterning is releasing now. All old frequencies, from this life or any other, this dimension or any other, are releasing now. Old frequencies, old conditioning, old energies from the past are letting go, releasing, and lifting.

Notice and allow. Keep letting go to allow the Divine Love.

Read slowly and pause between each sentence.

Divine Love is radiant within me now. Divine Love is increasing its presence within my energy field. The life energy of Divine Love is pulsating within my energy system now, in unison with the heartbeat of the Creator. I am radiant with Divine Love.

I am One with the fullness of Divine Mother's Love.

I am moving in the Wholeness of Divine Love as Divine Love creates more and more Love within me now.

Thank you Divine Mother, and so it is.

About Divine Love

With Divine Love you experience the world as harmonious and Whole. Divine Love brings you out of separation and into Oneness.

Divine Love Heals

When you use the Divine Love Tool, you are healing the issues of life with the most powerful energy in creation. Divine Love unites you with the Infinite, so the Infinite can pour Love into the challenges of your life. As Divine Love pours into your concerns, they transform. The Divine Love Tool heals the problems of life through your focused attention on filling them with Love.

Notice Divine Love

When you say the words of this Tool, intend to notice Divine Love. This Tool stirs a tangible flow of energy that you can identify as Divine Love.

Speak from Your Heart

Settle your attention in the heart as you speak the words, so that they come from your heart. Speak slowly and pause often so that the subtle energy of Divine Love can sink in.

Using Divine Love for Others

You can fill any person or situation with Divine Love. Just insert the person's name or the situation into the wording. For example, "Divine Love is pouring into my relationship now. My relationship is receiving Divine Love on every level." "_____ [name] is receiving Divine Love now ..."

Suggestions for Using Divine Love

Before any family gathering, intend to fill it with Divine Love. Inwardly, silently, shower your family with Divine Love. It will lift the family interactions into a harmonious, fun experience. If a tense situation arises, simply add more Divine Love and silently say "Go into the Light" to the negativity.

If you and your spouse have an argument, pour Divine Love in. It can settle the atmosphere and allow both of you to proceed without animosity.

Children can feel alone and rejected if their feelings are hurt by their friends. Pour in Divine Love to help them reclaim their sense of value.

Any time someone in your life is sad or depressed or is having a hard time, fill them with Divine Love. They will feel better and so will you.

Estranged relationships can be improved and often healed by pouring in Divine Love—into yourself, into the situation, and into the other person.

Divine Truth

Soften in the heart.

Pause for a moment after every sentence, and read slowly.

I am Whole and One with All That Is.

I accept the Divine Truth of my Infinite Wholeness now.

Wholeness of Divine Truth is awakening in my energy field. Wholeness of Divine Truth is filling me now. Wholeness of Divine Truth is opening throughout my energy system on every level of my life expression. Divine Truth knows only Oneness and is establishing the Truth of Oneness throughout my energy system now.

All untruth is letting go as Divine Truth fills my energy field with the Truth that I am Whole and One with God. Divine Truth is building the Presence of Truth in my energy system. This Presence of Truth is expanding and increasing Divine Truth throughout my physical and subtle fields.

I accept Divine Truth within me now on every level of my life expression.

All untruth anywhere in my multidimensional energy system is releasing, letting go, and changing into Truth. Divine Truth is Whole and complete within my energy system. I am healed by Truth. Truth allows Infinite Wholeness to be fully present within my energy system. Divine Truth carries wisdom and fills me with the Wisdom of Oneness now.

Truth is opening me into Wholeness again and again, freeing every place, point, and space in my energy field to vibrate Divine Truth. The untruth is collapsing now. Divine Truth is building a home of Truth within me, and I am healing in Wholeness of Divine Truth. Divine Truth is established within me now.

I accept the Divine Truth of my Infinite Wholeness now.

Finish with:

Thank you Divine Mother, and so it is.

About Divine Truth

The Divine Truth Healing Tool continues the process of moving you into complete union with your Divine Self. Far from being an intellectual concept, the Divine Truth of Oneness eventually becomes an experience that is never lost.

What Is Divine Truth?

There are many finite truths, true for a period of time. There is one Divine Truth that remains throughout time. The Divine Truth is that you are One with everything, and your True Self is Infinite and Whole. The Infinite You is permanent; the finite you continues to change.

Even though you might not have conscious awareness of this right now, the Truth is that you are Infinite and Whole. Life's evolution eventually awakens you to that recognition of your True Self.

What Does Divine Truth Do?

Using the Divine Truth Tool brings the power of Divine Truth to collapse all the lies and untruths you have accepted about yourself for lifetimes. Fear, shame, unworthiness, separation from God are revealed as lies when they face Divine Truth.

As you accept Divine Truth in your awareness, you begin to embrace seeming opposites as harmonious. You develop awareness of the Infinite in the finite, the Divine in material life. You become awakened, enlightened, experiencing the permanent Truth within, while continuing to be active in the relative field of change.

Results of the Divine Truth Tool

This Divine Mother Healing Tool builds in you the experience of your Wholeness and Oneness with God. As you say the words of Divine Truth, you awaken the Infinite Truth within your finite existence. Even though you may have forgotten, and believe you are small, limited, and imperfect, the Divine Truth is that you are powerful, unbounded, and perfect.

By using this Tool, you become highly discerning of the Truth or lack of Truth in your environment. This includes both in your own thoughts and feelings, and in the world outside of you. You become aware of the need to shift your thinking and align with the Divine Truth. This process helps you along your evolutionary path as you grow and change and unify with your Divine Nature.

Suggestions for Using Divine Truth

In business, it is easy to make a compromise with truth for the sake of profit. Use the Divine Truth Tool often to clarify issues of personal integrity.

Knowing the Divine Truth that you are Whole and One with God, even though you don't always consciously experience it, will give you tremendous self-confidence in all areas of your life.

When you have to make a decision and you are not sure of the right choice, the Divine Truth Tool connects you to the Truth within so you can come to the right decision.

Call upon Divine Truth when it is hard for you to tell the Truth, and it will give you the courage to be honest.

Ascending Light

Breathe into the heart.

Ascending Light is lifting me now. Ascending Light is pouring into my energy system. Ascending Light is moving throughout my multi-leveled energy field. Ascending Light is resonating on every level of my system, opening me to more Ascending Light. I accept Ascending Light within me now, in every aspect of my life expression.

I am radiant with Ascending Light and Ascending Light is increasing its presence within me moment by moment. I am being transformed in Ascending Light so that I may become all that I am capable of becoming.

Ascending Light is lifting and clearing all ancestral patterning within my energy system. Ascending Light is freeing my system from all limiting energies and frequencies. I allow Ascending Light to free me now.

Ascending Light is filling my cells. It is healing my cells as they vibrate with Ascending Light. More and more Ascending Light is saturating my cells now.

Breathe into the heart. Have the intention to soften and allow the Ascending Light.

Ascending Light is entering my DNA. Ascending Light is freeing my DNA and restructuring it in Divine Truth. My DNA is overflowing with Ascending Light. I am being lifted, opened, cleansed, and healed in Ascending Light. I am filling with Ascending Light. I am accepting Ascending Light, and it is transforming me now. I allow Ascending Light to fill me now.

I am lifted, opened, cleansed, and freed in Ascending Light now.

I am Whole. I am One with All That Is. I am filled with Ascending Light.

You can repeat this as often as you like to raise your vibration with Ascending Light.

Thank you Divine Mother, and so it is.

About Ascending Light

Ascending Light takes the refined energy gained throughout this healing sequence and further elevates it, enhancing and escalating the healing process for more profound transformation.

What Does Ascending Light Do?

Ascending Light lifts you into a very high vibrational frequency. It creates a vibration in your physical body that unites you with your Infinite Source.

The Ascending Light frequency allows the energies of your Divine purpose to come forth. Ascending Light creates the vibratory environment for your life purpose to express fully. Then the energies of your particular skills and abilities will resonate freely and express fully in your actions. It creates health and vitality in your physical body by accessing the ever-renewing energy available in your multi-leveled system.

What Is the Difference between Divine Light and Ascending Light?

Divine Light breaks up old, stuck frequencies and initiates deep healing. It's used to activate Light in the system for the purpose of transforming stuck energy into flowing energy. Then, Ascending Light lifts that flowing Light into more refinement.

Use Divine Light to break through existing patterns and conditioning. It's recommended to start with Divine Light because it heals and transforms your system. Use Ascending Light later in the healing sequence, after clearing your energy system of blocks. Ascending Light then lifts your system's frequencies further, refining and polishing the quality of light in your vibrational field.

Suggestions for Using Ascending Light

When you need a lift out of the quandaries of daily life, bring in Ascending Light. It will elevate you to a place of freedom where you can have an experience of lightness and can gain a new perspective.

When you feel heavy, dull energy, either within yourself or from the people around you, bring in Ascending Light to lift out of it.

Use Ascending Light every day to keep your vibration on a very high level where the negative, dense, and lower frequencies cannot bring you down.

Cutting Binding Ties

Breathe into the heart.

> **I ask Divine Mother and Archangel Michael with his Blue Flame Sword of Truth to lovingly cut all binding ties, hooks, threads, cords, attachments, and any other kind of tie that may be limiting me in any way.**

> **These ties are now cut between myself and _____ [name].** (Name specific persons, places, events, situations, or conditions where you have felt limited, bound, or attached in any way. If you are completing a full healing sequence, cut ties between yourself and everything that has been released during the healing session.)

Then say:

> **These binding ties, hooks, threads, cords, and attachments are now lovingly cut by Archangel Michael and his Blue Flame Sword of Truth. They are completely and thoroughly cut, lifted, healed, removed, dissolved, and released from every level of my multi-leveled energy field.**

Next say:

> **I ask Divine Mother and Archangel Michael to release all these ties and attachments from me now, layer, by layer, by layer.**

> **I allow these binding ties and attachments to be let go and transmuted into Light by Divine Mother now, layer, by layer, by layer.**

> **These ties are lovingly cut layer, by layer, by layer, by layer, by layer, by layer, by layer throughout my entire vibrational field.**

Image the ties being cut.

> **Even the subtlest ties are cut, lifted, healed, released, and dissolved layer, by layer, by layer, by layer.**

Repeat:

> **They are cut layer, by layer, by layer, by layer …**

… until you sense the release is complete. The repetition is important because you are cutting ties through every level of your multi-leveled energy system.

Then say:

I am free.

Finish with:

**I know that I am Whole and One with All That Is.
Thank you Divine Mother, and so it is.**

About Cutting Binding Ties

Why Do We Cut Binding Ties?

Cutting binding ties breaks the unhealthy energy attachments between you and other people, thoughts, or situations. Many connections are normal and comfortable. "Binding" ties are those that inhibit your Self-expression and constrict your life force.

When Do We Cut Binding Ties?

Cut binding ties whenever you notice that you can't be yourself. Perhaps you are dominated by an individual or a group, or you feel manipulated or controlled by another. In all these cases, your energy is unconsciously tied to their energy field. You have given up the freedom to be yourself. Cutting the binding ties frees you to live the truth of who you are with everyone.

After a Divine Mother healing session, cut ties with everything that has been healed and released, to assure there is a clean release of the discordant energies that were constricting you.

In daily life, you can cut ties with anything you can't get out of your mind—a person, book, movie, relationship, an incident, or something in the news. This indicates that your mind has become energetically bound to these things, so release yourself by cutting the subtle ties.

If you wake up at night with a nightmare, cutting ties with the nightmare will help you relax and go back to sleep.

Why Would I Cut Binding Ties with People I Love?

By cutting binding ties with your loved ones, you free all involved to be themselves. Then the relationships can be honest, interesting, and liberating, instead of predictable, tedious, and irritating. You cut the *binding* ties, those ties that capture and hold you to a small identity in the relationship. You are not cutting the deep, loving connection between you; in fact, cutting the binding ties opens you to deeper love. Genuine love can never be cut.

Suggestions for Using Cutting Binding Ties

If you are living for another person and not for yourself, cut binding ties with them. Cutting ties will free you to be yourself without guilt. Then you can enjoy each other much more and build mutual respect.

When you can't get your mind off a movie you have seen or a book you are reading, cut ties with it. It will free your attention to be in the moment.

If you are part of a group that is judging you harshly, cut ties between yourself and the group. This will relieve the pain you feel about their criticism, and you can stop caring what they think of you.

If you have a friend who is constantly coming to you with their problems, and you are feeling very responsible for helping them, cut ties between you. This will let you feel less attached to their life issues and now you can approach them in a more expanded way.

Cutting ties with a parent and all your past issues will take you out of the role of dependent child. You can then relate to the parent as an independent adult.

Divine Grace

Breathe into the heart.

The Wholeness of Divine Grace is completely filling my energy field now. Divine Grace is pouring into my energy field now, filling every place in my multi-leveled energy system with the presence of Divine Grace. Divine Grace is opening more Grace in my energy system, completely immersing me in the presence of Divine Grace.

I accept Divine Grace within me now on every level of my life expression.

Divine Grace is permeating, penetrating, and saturating my energy field with the Holy Presence of Divine Grace. Divine Grace is opening within every particle, atom, molecule, cell, point, place, and space within my entire energy field now.

More and more Wholeness of Divine Grace is filling me again and again. Wholeness of Divine Grace is pouring more Divine Grace into me now. I am lifted, opened, cleansed, and freed in the Wholeness of Divine Grace.

Divine Grace is opening again and again into me and into all areas of my life and gracing my entire energy field.

Divine Grace is bathing me on all levels of my life expression. Divine Grace is renewing and sustaining me in a life blessed with Divine Grace.

I am living in Divine Grace as I move through my life. I am lifted, opened, cleansed, and freed in Divine Grace.

Divine Grace is opening again and again within me now and gracing my entire existence. My life is now operating under the law of Divine Grace. I am now opening in Wholeness, moving in Grace, opening in Wholeness, moving in Grace.

Thank you Divine Mother, and so it is.

About Divine Grace

After all the transformation that has occurred in the process of using these Healing Tools, Divine Grace comes forth to bless you.

What Is Divine Grace?

Divine Grace is beyond reason and logic. It is Grace when something wonderful happens that you do not understand. Divine Grace made it happen. Grace surprises the mind, intellect, and ego. Divine Grace is the universe generously supporting you.

What Does Divine Grace Do?

Divine Grace polishes the sculpture that is the "new you." You have done the chopping, carving, and digging out. Then you have filed and buffed and smoothed, and now you put on the luster that makes your life glow. Divine Grace is the vibrational frequency that makes life glow, that creates a special sheen in your heart and soul. It is a spiritual quality that cannot be described because it is so sublime. With the Divine Grace technique, sublime energy takes over, allowing your life to be conducted under a new set of laws—the laws of Divine Grace, which allow beauty and wisdom to infuse your awareness.

At this stage of the vibrational healing sequence, there is an opportunity to receive profound wisdom from deep within. You have done all the clearing work and are now in a position where it may be natural and easy to receive Divine Wisdom.

What Is the Law of Divine Grace?

Grace uses a deeper set of laws that are not understood by the linear thinking mind. There is no explanation for Grace other than the Divine Hand at work.

The law of Divine Grace is the guarantee that you are always supported by the universe. That support takes the form of giving you your highest good in every situation.

Living under the law of Divine Grace allows you to live innocently, without fear. When you live under the law of Divine Grace, you live in the Oneness of all life, where you are aware that everything in existence serves and supports you.

What Is the Effect of Divine Grace?

As you grow in Grace, life becomes gentler, easier, and smoother. The universe supports you at all times, but when, through Grace, you have grown to know and experience its unconditional Love and support, it appears to serve you even more. Divine Grace reveals the majesty of Mother God in intimate personal relationship with you.

Suggestions for Using Divine Grace

If you ever find yourself in a situation that feels so overwhelming that you can't see how you can get through it, bring in Divine Grace. It opens you to Divine possibilities.

Simply saying "Grace, Grace, Grace" in any situation will help you to let go, so that Divine Grace can intervene.

Using the Divine Grace Tool can help you feel empowered and embraced by the Divine and help you trust in the goodness of life.

Closing a Divine Mother Healing Session

Breathe into your heart and say:

> **Thank you, Divine Mother and all the Beings of Wholeness, for the purification and alignment with Truth that I have received from you today.**

> **My heart is open and receiving your Divine Presence. I am moving with you through this day.**

> **The Love that you have for me is now resonating throughout my body, mind, and heart as I conduct my life in alignment with Divine Truth.**

> **I now allow Divine Love to flow into my physical body as I become active and engaged with the environment.**

Begin to gently move and stretch, slowly bringing the body from a resting state into activity.

> **I come into activity balanced and integrated with my physical surroundings.**

> **I know that Divine Mother is with me and that all is well.**

Say the following affirmations, speaking with confidence, knowing that it is so:

> **I am alert. I am clear. I am balanced within myself and with my outer environment.**

> **I am Whole. I am One with All That Is. I am divinely protected by Divine Mother's Love.**

> **I close all doors, openings, and holes in my energy field to the limited planes of existence now.**

> **I close to the astral plane** (pause a moment and say, "Close"); **to the limited extra-terrestrial regions, "Close"; to the inter-dimensional realms, "Close"; to the lost souls, "Close"; to the false gods, "Close"; to the negative thought forms, "Close"; to the heavy, dense energy beings, "Close"; and to the race-mind consciousness of Mother Earth, "Close." All doors, openings, holes to these regions are now closed and sealed in the name and through the power of Divine Mother.**

Image doors closing around you.

Then say:

My aura and body of light are radiant with Divine Presence.

Pause for a moment here to fill the aura with the Light. Sense, feel, know, image, and intend that your auric field, for about ten feet all around you, is brilliant with Light, sparkling with Light, glowing with Light, empowered and vibrant with Divine Light.

Then say:

I am aligned with Truth.
I am Whole.

End with three grounding breaths:

Take a deep breath into your body, bringing all of the Divine Love, Light, Truth, and Grace to fill your physical body, and then as you exhale, connect with Mother Earth by sending the energy into Mother Earth beneath your feet. Again, take another deep breath, bringing the Divine Energy into your body and exhale into Mother Earth. Then take one more breath, filling the physical body with Divine Energy, and as you exhale, ground yourself on Mother Earth.

Now say:

I am now moving through my life with Grace, Power, and Divine Integrity.
Thank you Divine Mother, and so it is.

Take any additional time you need to stretch, open your eyes slowly, and integrate with the environment.

About Closing a Divine Mother Healing Session

Closing the session is very important, so don't skip this step.

Why Do We Come Out of the Session Slowly?

At the end of the session, it is essential that you give your body time to switch gears, to become more active in the outer world. This should be an easy and comfortable transition both physically and energetically. It's important to be grounded on the physical plane in order to integrate and maintain the Divine vibration.

By using these Tools, you have opened deeply into the home of Divine Mother at the subtlest level of creation and from there, moved in and out of creation's Infinite Source. This caused many issues to be released. You are in a different place now physically, emotionally, mentally, and spiritually. Coming out slowly allows time to integrate the "new you" into all levels of your active life.

What Does the Closing Do?

Having used the Healing Tools, you are now coming back into activity with more clarity, strength, and Wholeness. It's a delicate transition period. The Closing process assures that your energy field stays clear, radiant with Light, and resilient to anything that might attempt to dismantle the strength of your newly empowered vibrational system.

This Closing now moves you into other activities of life with a declaration of gratitude to the Divine, and with trust in your Infinite Self. This process assists you in making a smooth transition into activity, centered and empowered in your Divine Nature.

If you have not taken enough time to do the Closing thoroughly, you might feel roughness, agitation, a headache, or feel spaced-out. Closing a healing session gently and completely will help you to come out centered, stable, and connected with your heart. The Closing will ground you and bring all the benefits of the healing very solidly into your life.

So be kind to yourself by not skipping this important step.

Why Do We Strengthen the Aura?

A strong auric field around your body resists discord from the environment. You have just released much of the discord you had accumulated in your energy system. Now it's important to stay clear. Agitation, negativity, or conflict from the environment can enter a weak aura to create discomfort and confusion. Closing and strengthening your aura fortifies it to support what you have gained during the healing session.

Why Say the Aura Is Radiant with Divine Presence?

You say this to acknowledge the Divine Beings who are now very attentive to you and want to help you in your life. It reminds you of your union with the Divine and the close association you have with Divine Mother at all times.

Chapter 8

Specialized Tools and Explanations

Self-Love Exercise

Call yourself by name, and say inwardly:

> **I love you, _____ [your name]. You are beautiful. I love you with all my heart. You are perfect in my eyes. You are wonderful. I love everything about you. You are good. You are wise. You are dear to me.**

> **You are _____**

Continue with more compliments. Engage your heart; speak to yourself from your heart. Say what you want to hear; for example:

> **You are kind. You are loving. You are capable. You are smart. You are strong. You are generous. You are fun to be with. You are thoughtful. You are honest. You care about people. You are creative. You are graceful. You are worthy. You are joyful. You are brilliant. You are radiant with Light. You are courageous.**

Don't qualify what you are saying by adding, "You are loveable when you are nice to people" or "You are good some of the time." Love all parts of yourself without qualification or justification.

Each person may wish to hear something different; tailor your words to what is meaningful to you.

Often negative or self-critical thoughts come up during the practice. If this happens, go into your heart and stand up for yourself. Don't allow yourself to be bullied by critical thoughts. Say from the conviction of your heart, "That's not true—I am good, I am honest, I am kind, I am loving," or other appropriate words. Your heart is where your courage is. Speak from the heart and the critical mind will back off. Don't accept any criticism or argument from the intellect/ego/mind. If it persists, say, "In the name of God, I command you to go into the Light."

Continue speaking to yourself lovingly, complimenting yourself by saying the things that you wish your partner, family member, employer, or best friend would say to you. You know what you want them to say. Say it to yourself. It will deeply nourish you.

Continue speaking these loving words until you become relaxed and receptive to them in your heart. Let them soak in and nurture your whole being.

Notice the good feeling that is generated. Sink into it, melt into it, and let it embrace you. Become the good feeling you have created.

As you melt and let go, you become softened and expanded. Continue the process until you feel relaxed, safe, and loved.

Tips for Getting Started

If you're having difficulty with this exercise:

1. Pretend Divine Mother is saying the words to you. She loves you unconditionally.
2. Pretend somebody who cares deeply for you is saying these words.
3. What you are saying does not have to make logical sense. You don't have to give reasons to prove what you are saying. (For example: "I'm good because I gave money to the homeless." Just say, "I am good.")
4. Don't get stuck in details. You want this to flow. Talk from your heart, not your mind. The heart has no need for details or proof.
5. If the negative self-talk is so strong that it's hard to get past it, then use other Divine Mother Tools like the Go Command or the Break Command. You may even need a personal healing session from a trained Divine Mother Healing practitioner.
6. Record yourself speaking the words of self-love. Play it any time. It is especially effective when heard before going to sleep at night and when awakening in the morning.
7. Begin by using the Creating the Flow of Love Exercise to get the love flowing between you and Divine Mother. Then shift into saying to yourself, "I love you _____ [your name]" and continue with the Self-Love Exercise.

About the Self-Love Exercise

What Is the Self-Love Exercise?

This exercise reminds you of who you really are. You are a Divine Being, infinitely loved and infinitely worthy to be loved. The Truth needs to be spoken so that you can live it. When you make statements that acknowledge your value, you start living in the dignity of your True Self. This exercise unites you with your True Self, which is also your Divine Self.

The heart is craving to hear the Truth about you. Others do not acknowledge you enough.

You must acknowledge yourself. The Self-Love Exercise gives you the strength to accept the Truth of your goodness and to stop accepting the lies. We live in a climate of criticism. People have criticized you for years, and you have accepted that criticism, even though it hurts. You have even learned to criticize yourself and that hurts more. Somewhere inside, you know it is false, and you want to hear the Truth. This exercise empowers you in the Truth of your innate goodness, which is your God-ness, so that you can live the power of that in daily life.

Why Should I Use It?

It is important to love yourself. Too much self-criticism damages your physical body. Your system responds to every thought you have by expanding or contracting. Negative self-talk contracts your system. This contraction is damaging—it blocks your life force. It is time to end the negative self-talk. Self-love expands your system, increasing the flow of your life force, giving you greater health, vitality, and self-confidence.

How Do I Use It?

Just soften and let your heart talk. Your heart knows the Truth of who you are. Bring your attention to your heart area, allowing the words to come from there. This exercise is deceptively simple. Though simple to practice, it has a great power to change your everyday life. Be innocent.

When Do I Use This Exercise?

A great time to use this exercise is at night while in bed before going to sleep. When you are under the covers and settling down, it's an intimate time to talk to yourself. You are more receptive to love when your body is relaxing and your mind is becoming quiet.

Other times to use this exercise are after meditation or prayer, when awakening in the morning, or while enjoying nature. Use it on occasions when you need self-confidence, like when preparing for a business presentation, audition, speech, interview, hosting a party, or anytime you are nervous.

How Do I Benefit from This Exercise?

As you speak kindly and lovingly to yourself, you start to soften and accept that you are worthy of love and you are lovable. You comfort your heart, healing the pain of criticism and rejection. Over time your life will change. As you consistently practice, you will no longer let yourself or anyone else belittle you.

When you increase self-appreciation, you attract friends, lovers, co-workers, and life partners who love and appreciate you.

Practicing this exercise reminds you of who you really are: a good person with good intentions.

You begin to step out of fear and remember that you are a Divine Being in a physical form, full of Light and Love.

Suggestions for Using the Self-Love Exercise

If you fall into self-criticism, dissolve those negative words with statements of self-love and self-value to change the vibration the criticism has created.

Practice telling yourself all the things you wish other people would notice in you. This helps you feel deeply loved, not only by you, but by God and the universe. Acknowledging your good qualities will help you step into them in daily life. You will have a new sense of confidence coming from your new feelings of self-worth, initiated by the nice things you say to yourself.

Call yourself and leave a message on your own voice mail. Say positive things like "I love you. You are great. You are the best, etc." Leave it on your voice mail and listen to it every day.

Keep going with this exercise! You can never hear enough about how good you are. It is something private, beautiful, and very healing that you can give to yourself.

Creating the Flow of Love

This is an exchange of love between you and Divine Mother.

Instructions from Divine Mother:

I want you to activate the flow of Love between us. Be Me. At the deepest level of your life, we are One, so it is okay to "pretend" to be Me. I want you to use your inner voice and speak My words of love to yourself, either out loud or silently.

Pretending to be Me, say in your voice:

I love you, _____ [your name].

Then, as yourself, say back to Me:

I love you, Divine Mother.

I say in your voice:

I love you, _____ [your name].

Notice the effect of that statement inside of you. It is very subtle, but you <u>can</u> notice My love.

Now, I want you to say that back to Me:

I love you, Divine Mother.

And notice the love flowing to Me, like a wave on the ocean. We will exchange "I love you's."

You say in your voice, being Me:

I love you, _____ [your name].

Then say, being you:

I love you, Divine Mother.

Notice the energy ebbing and flowing between us.

Continue saying **"I love you, _____** [your name], **I love you, Divine Mother, I love you, _____** [your name], **I love you, Divine Mother ...,"** speaking back and forth this way until you feel drenched in My love and connected to Me. This is a way to activate our personal relationship.

The purpose of this exercise is to get the flow of love moving between us strongly enough so that you can feel it.

If you feel any resistance or mental objections when you do this exercise, use the Go Command or Break Command to dissolve the resistance. Keep coming back to the "I love you's."

About Creating the Flow of Love

What Is the Purpose of This Exercise?

This exercise activates your personal relationship with Divine Mother. She truly wants a personal relationship with you because this is how She can help you the most. This exercise creates an exchange of love between you and Divine Mother. It creates a wave of love flowing between you. The flow of love is the most important thing in any personal relationship. When love stops flowing, the relationship becomes stagnant.

In this exercise, Divine Mother and you consciously create the flow of the most powerful energy in the universe, Love. It lifts you, heals you, frees you, and enriches this most important relationship.

What If I Can't Get the Flow Going?

Feeling any resistance or mental objections when doing this exercise calls for using the Go Command or Break Command to dissolve the resistance. Ask for Divine Mother's help as you say "Go" and "Break" to heal the blocks in your system and get the flow going.

It's very subtle, but you *can* notice Divine Mother's love. It becomes more tangible after a minute or two of practicing the exercise.

Can I Speak for Divine Mother?

At the deepest level of your life, you and Divine Mother are One, so it's okay to "imagine" that Divine Mother is saying "I love you." Eventually, you will feel Her presence and know She is, in fact, saying the words.

How to Deepen the Flow of Love

Soften more deeply and allow the words to flow from your heart. Let the sound of the words resonate through your whole chest and torso. Let the vibration of what you're saying become alive in you as if your cells are saying it.

Suggestions for Creating the Flow of Love

Driving alone in your car is a good time to use this exchange of love with Divine Mother. It will remind you that Divine Mother is always in the car with you. This can make a long drive really fun.

Any time you feel down, creating the flow of love with Divine Mother will comfort you and lift you back on your feet. With Divine Mother, you will no longer feel so alone.

Heart Exercise – Long Form

Read this with the intention to do it as you read.

Breathe into the heart center, not just the heart organ, but the whole chest area. Breathe as if the breath is coming through the front of the chest into the heart and soften in the heart to receive the breath. Allow the heart to open, like a flower opening its petals, to receive the warm, soft breath.

If it is difficult to keep your attention in the heart, take many strong, slow, deep breaths (10 to 15) into the chest area. The deep breaths quiet mental activity and then it's easier to focus attention on the heart.

The breath carries life energy. Soften in the heart as it receives the breath, and notice the flow of breath moving into the heart center.

Continue to put your attention on the heart center, which is the whole chest area, not just the heart organ. Notice if there is any tightness or discomfort there. If there is, breathe into it, allowing the breath to flow through it, opening it up, and moving the stream of breath through the discomfort. Continue this process until the discomfort dissolves.

If there is no discomfort, breathe into whatever you notice there, whether it's physical, emotional, visual, or vibrational.

When the discomfort dissolves, or when the experience changes, notice what presents next in the heart. Whatever you notice, breathe into it.

If you do not notice anything, breathe into the "nothing" and notice the movement of breath flowing into the "nothing."

Layers of the heart will unfold as you continue the exercise, revealing deeper blocks or deeper clarity depending on whether your heart is blocked or open. Keep noticing what presents. Even if it is a comfortable or pleasant sensation, breathe into that. Everything that presents is asking you to breathe into it. You are healing and awakening your heart by opening it to the flow of life energy carried on the breath. This flow not only releases and dissolves blocks to the movement of life energy through your heart, it also connects you to your True Self. These blocks have kept your heart constricted, tense, and disconnected from your True Self.

The process is as follows:

1. Breathe into the heart center.
2. What do you notice?

3. Breathe into whatever you notice until it changes.
4. When it changes, notice what presents next, and breathe into that.
5. Continue breathing into whatever the heart presents. There will be layers of the heart unfolding as you breathe into it.
6. This can continue for as long as desired, but it's best if you proceed until there is a sense of peace.

This is the Heart Exercise. Practice it often, for as long as you can, eyes closed in quiet times or eyes open in activity. Some people use the heart exercise as a meditation; others use it as a relaxation technique. Doing it for a few minutes or even seconds can center you and provide comfort and peace.

About the Heart Exercise – Long Form

Why Is It Important to Practice the Heart Exercise?

During your lifetimes on earth, your heart has been wounded. This has caused your heart to try to protect itself by constricting and setting up shields. You cannot express your full potential when your heart is constricted and shielded. Your Divine Self is located in your heart. The Heart Exercise releases blocks that constrict your heart and separate you from the experience of your Divine Self. This is a practice for opening the heart, releasing its pain, and experiencing yourself as Infinite, Whole, and One with God.

How Does the Heart Exercise Work?

The constrictions in your heart are released by using the breath. The breath carries life force. When life force is allowed to flow through the heart, it moves through the blocks, dissolving them.

Breathing into your heart is not only effective for dissolving blocks, but also for uniting with the Divine. At first, the blocks must be dissolved because they are covering the deeper layers of the heart. Once your heart is clear and open, continue to breathe into whatever you notice there, and you will begin to experience your Divine Self.

When Do I Use the Heart Exercise?

Use it every time you become worried, frustrated, nervous, or distressed. It will calm you in any circumstance, whether you are alone or in a group. When those around you are upset, use it so that you can remain calm. You can do it wherever you are, in a car, a business meeting, a family confrontation, at night when you can't sleep, or to settle yourself into prayer or meditation. The Heart Exercise centers you in the place of Wisdom and Truth so that you can easily manage every situation in your life.

A shortened form of the Heart Exercise is used at the beginning of the Divine Mother Healing

Tool sequence. It's also used before many of the Tools to keep you centered in the heart as you go through the vibrational healing sequence.

What Are the Benefits of Using This Exercise?

The heart has access to the Infinite Mind of God. When you are centered in the heart, you are using Divine Intelligence. You are calm and peaceful, yet dynamic in activity. You influence others by creating harmony around you. You experience God residing in your heart.

Suggestions for Using the Heart Exercise

If you are in a business meeting where there is disagreement, breathe into your heart. It will calm you and everyone else at the meeting as well. This practice is useful for any kind of gathering.

If you ever receive a call from someone who is very agitated or anxious, guide that person into the Heart Exercise. Guide them to breathe into their heart as you breathe into yours. It will calm you both and change the situation. Then you can discuss options for their challenge.

Getting a big bill in the mail that you feel you can't afford to pay can cause tremendous anxiety. Start breathing into the heart area. Breathing into the tension in your chest will help to relax you and center you in your heart. The wisdom of the heart can then come forth to present you with new ideas for managing the situation.

You may use the Heart Exercise as a simple meditation for calming and centering yourself.

Spinning Ascending Light

You can transform the energy of any uncomfortable experience by spinning Ascending Light in it. The spiraling Light lifts your vibrational frequency out of density. Density is often experienced as depression, fear, unworthiness, hopelessness, helplessness, or despair. You can be lifted with the Ascending Light spiral out of these experiences. It takes focus and attention. Here is the process:

Breathe into your heart and soften there.

Allow a spiral of Ascending Light to spin in any area of density. Spin it in the places where you are feeling heavy, dense, dull, or stuck. Expressions of these conditions often appear as pain, frustration, self-criticism, negative thoughts, or hostility. If you want to lift the vibration of your whole physical body, spin Light in the whole body.

You can imagine, picture, see, sense, or feel the spiral spinning like a whirlwind or tornado of Light.

Don't be concerned about the direction of the spin, clockwise or counter-clockwise. The spin will spontaneously take the direction that is most needed for your support. The Divine Mind knows how to facilitate your intention to spin Ascending Light.

See, feel, or just know that the spiral is present and spinning upward.
Once you get the spiral going, allow it to spin faster and faster.
Then spin the Light even faster ... like a golden tornado, constantly accelerating its velocity.

The spiral of Ascending Light is lifting you and freeing you from all dense, heavy vibrational frequencies.

Spin faster ...
Accelerate the speed ...
Accelerate faster ...

Continue to accelerate the spin faster again and again ...

Soften and relax while you spin, keeping the attention on the spin while staying open and alert. Be easy with no strain. Keep softening anywhere in your system that starts to tense or strain. If you ever start to get a headache, soften and breathe into the heart.

Spin the Light for as long as it takes until the density is lifted and the stuck energy is freed. You will eventually notice a shift. Until then, keep accelerating the spin.

It can take some time, but when the stuck energy breaks there is an expansion, a sense of freedom, and a letting go.

Finish with:

Thank you Divine Mother, and so it is.

About Spinning Ascending Light

Why Do We Spin Ascending Light?

Spinning Ascending Light is used to dissolve density and lift vibrational frequency. Imagine it spinning upward like a corkscrew, a spiral of swirling Light, or a miniature tornado of Light.

Each person creates a universe around them. We all have our individual universes. Spinning Ascending Light is like creating a new universe. The old universe needs to be upgraded.

The universe of a depressed person is filled with very contracting energies, continuously stifling life force. When someone is living in contraction, suppression, and depression, their universe is contracting.

Upgrade your universe by spinning the Ascending Light rapidly through your body, in your heart, in your third eye, and in your other chakras. This keeps you expanding like the larger universe, the interstellar universe, so that you continue to access your creative resources and move them into action to support your life.

Work with the spiral of Ascending Light frequently, and you'll find that you consistently break through the pain of contraction and give the universe your dynamism.

Why Do We Accelerate the Speed?

Accelerating the speed of the spinning Light continuously raises the vibration higher and higher. It breaks the old frequencies and lifts whatever you are focused upon into freedom, lightness, and the highest Truth. It sustains expansion, and allows new frequencies to be drawn forth into your life.

The acceleration of the spin impacts your physical form, refining your body at the atomic, subatomic, and energy levels. This helps you step out of the suffering that has dominated material life on earth. As higher frequency energies engage with you, more joy, pleasure, peace, and freedom open in your life.

Where Do We Spin the Light?

Spin Light in any person, group, place, or condition that has become negative, dull, stuck, depressed, or otherwise compromised. You can spin Light in your whole energy system, in your body, in your chakras, or in any single chakra, in an organ, or any place that needs support. You can spin Light in a person who is ill to lift their vibration. Spin Light in any situation that feels heavy or immovable. Be creative with your spinning Light. You will lighten up life.

Suggestions for Using Spinning Light

If you are attending a meeting or are part of a group that descends into disagreements and hostility, start to spin Light in the whole room. This helps everyone to let go of their rigidity, and agreements can be reached.

Whenever you notice someone who is looking distressed or unhappy, spin Light in that person. Sometimes you may feel that a whole room is heavy and dense. In that situation, spin Light in the whole room. Remember that you can lift vibration anywhere by spinning Light there.

Anytime you notice a stuck heaviness in your heart, allow Light to spin in the heaviness. Don't stop till the heaviness breaks. Afterwards you will feel more light and joyful.

Aura Empowerment

Breathe into the heart.

As you say this Aura Empowerment technique, see, feel, know, image, or intend that the Light is doing what you are saying during every statement.

> **My aura, the space around my body for at least 10 feet in all directions, is filled with Light. Divine Light beams from my core and fills my auric field, like the rays of a brilliant sun.**
>
> **I am radiant with Light. My aura is sparkling with Light, brilliant with Light, glowing with Light, blazing with Light.**

Continue to image this while saying it. Notice it, feel it, see it, know it.

> **My auric field is vibrant with Divine Light and alive with life force. Divine Light is radiating from my core. It protects me and creates a shield of Light within me and around me wherever I go and in whatever I do.**
>
> **It remains powerful and strong as I interact with others. Nothing limited can penetrate the power of my auric field. It is holding me in a place of safety.**

Notice the Light and feel the safety.

> **I am Whole. The power in me comes from my Infinite Source.**
> **I am One with All That Is.**
> **Thank you Divine Mother, and so it is.**

Note: As an added protection at any time, you can revisit the Closing Holes in Your Aura Tool on page 55 to firmly close your aura to all limited subtle energies.

About Aura Empowerment

Why Do I Need a Powerful Aura?

Your aura is an energy field that surrounds and supports your body. A strong aura keeps the mind clear and the body healthy. A weak aura allows the mind to become confused, fearful, angry, despairing, and disturbed and the body to become vulnerable to illness. Your aura is designed to protect your body and mind. It shields you from negative influences in the environment. A weak aura is the biggest problem most people have because it allows the strength of their True Self to be undermined and weakened by outside energies, usually without them being aware of it.

When Do I Need to Empower My Aura?

Empower your aura often, at least every morning before facing the day. Empower your aura during the day when feeling influenced, pressured, or controlled by something or someone else.

Empower your aura when entering an environment of stress or emotional intensity such as hospitals, airports, or any large crowd. If you often have nightmares or disturbed sleep, empower your aura before going to bed. Use the Aura Empowerment many times a day, and soon the brilliant Light of your aura will be "switched on" all the time.

What Weakens the Aura?

Negative thoughts, self-criticism, and acceptance of the criticism of others can weaken your aura. It is also weakened by the use of alcohol, drugs, cigarettes, and all addictions. Your aura becomes frail when you give your personal power to another. Illness can open and weaken an aura. Consistent empowerment of your aura and using the Divine Mother Tools reverses these conditions.

How Does the Aura Empowerment Work?

The power of Divine Light raises the vibratory frequency of your aura. The Divine Light frequencies lift you out of the discord and confusion of lower frequencies. Your aura becomes powerful and brilliant as you regularly enliven the Divine Light within you with the use of these Tools. Your aura then emanates the power of your Highest Self as you claim your Oneness with God. An empowered aura automatically repels negativity in the environment.

Suggestions for Using the Aura Empowerment

When you feel overly sensitive and off-balance, use the Aura Empowerment along with Divine Mother's other Tools to keep yourself physically strong and self-confident. The Aura Empowerment helps prevent you from being thrown off center by the outer world.

If you meet people who unload their anger and frustration on you, power up your aura. They are passing negative energies on to you, and a strong aura protects you. By regularly empowering your aura, you will find these experiences occurring less and less frequently.

Empower your aura daily to maintain a strong field of protection from negativity and discord as you go through your daily activities.

Canceling Spells and Curses

Breathe into your heart and center there.

Step 1:

Fortify yourself by calling on your Divine Friends from the Invocation of Divine Beings. Create the Protective Sphere of Light from the Invocation around you, with Archangel Michael standing on all sides of you. Then use the Closing Holes in Your Aura technique. Now you are strong, centered, and held by Divine Mother.

Step 2:

Say out loud in a firm voice and with conviction:

> **I ask Divine Mother, Archangel Michael, Jesus Christ, and the Company of Heaven, to cancel and release all spells, enchantments, curses, oaths, hexes, sorcery, pacts, bindings, and the like, and all dark magic that I may have ever been a part of, either given or received, in my multidimensional existence, in all former lifetimes either on this planet or in any other domain or dimension.**

Step 3:

Then declare with the power of Divine authority:

> **These are all now dissolved, released, canceled, broken, made null and void in the name and through the power of Jesus Christ, in the name and through the power of Archangel Michael, in the name and through the power of Divine Mother.**

Say firmly, pausing after each command:

> **They are all now broken ... shattered ... smashed ... dismantled ... dissolved, made null and void ...**

> **And all subtle negative entities holding them in place must go into the Light! ... Go, Break, Go, Break, Shatter, Smash ...**

Repeat the commands **"Break! Shatter! Dissolve!"** and **"Go into the Light!"** again and again. You are healing layer after layer of the spell or curse. Keep going until you feel openness and expansion in your energy.

Go back and repeat this Divine Mother Tool from the beginning, three or four times as needed, consistently calling on the support of your Divine Friends, and reading all the way through to the "Break" and "Go" section.

The effectiveness of this Tool is in its repetitions, as deeper and deeper layers of the spell or curse are being broken.

Step 4:

After a period of saying **"Break"** and **"Go,"** test whether the negative energy has cleared. See the list of different types of spells and curses below. One by one, go over each to see if any of them still has a "charge" or an "agitated vibration" attached to it. If yes, continue to use **"Go!"** and **"Break!"** numerous times for that particular one. When the curse, spell, or oath is neutralized, there will no longer be a "charge" around it, only peace.

Check for a "charge" from each word below by saying:

I ask Divine Mother to heal all _____ [name spell type].

Then pause and hold the word in your awareness determining if it is clear. Go through the list and heal where still needed until all words are completely neutral with no vibrational agitation around them.

List:

> **Spells** ... heal if necessary with the Go and Break Commands.
> **Enchantments** ... heal if necessary.
> **Curses** ... heal if necessary.
> **Oaths** ... heal if necessary.
> **Hexes** ... heal if necessary.
> **Sorcery** ... heal if necessary.
> **Pacts** ... heal if necessary.
> **Bindings and the like** ... heal if necessary.
> **All dark magic** ... heal if necessary.

Important:

Repeat **"Break"** and **"Go"** emphatically after each one until you are certain that the energy has been dissolved and the vibration broken for each negative issue. Keep letting go into the Infinite Source, softening as you do this.

When you are satisfied that all the words in this list are free of negative charge, continue to heal your energy field by reading the following Healing Tools in the order listed:

Divine Nectar
Ascending Light
Closing Holes in Your Aura
Binding Tie Cut - Cut the ties to everything that has been healed.
Divine Grace
Aura Empowerment

Then end with:

Thank you Divine Mother, and so it is.

Note: If you don't feel completely cleared, go through the entire Divine Mother Healing Tool sequence from beginning to end. It will lift your vibration out of the realm of these issues.

If you desire assistance, Divine Mother certified practitioners are available at www. DivineMotherOnline.net.

About Canceling Spells and Curses

When Do I Cancel Spells and Curses?

Use this Divine Mother Tool any time you sense someone's purposeful misuse of power to weaken, control, manipulate, or use you. Sensing that you need this Tool may come as an intuition, an unusual sensation in the body, or an old memory. Even if you are not sure it's a sign of a spell or curse, go ahead and use this Tool to clear it. It's better to use it unnecessarily than to ignore a situation that could be presenting for healing. And definitely, if you know you have had a spell or curse put on you, that is when to use this Tool.

Canceling Strong Negative Intentions in Everyday Life

A strong negative thought or statement activates destructive energy. It behaves like a curse or negative oath. The energy of it is damaging. If someone has hurled a negative oath of harmful intent at you or made a vow to harm you, the energy of that needs to be broken. If you have made statements against someone else, fueled by the power of strong negative emotion, use this Tool to dismantle that energy.

The power of these statements has caused massive harm over the centuries and kept the human race locked in a cycle of revenge and pain. You can break this cycle.

Why Repeat This Tool Several Times?

This Tool clears and transmutes very negative energies that attempt to usurp your free will and self-authority. These intense vibrations take hold on many levels of your system. Repeating this treatment numerous times with firm conviction breaks the energy and dissolves this strong vibration on every level. A strong negative vibration could take five to twenty minutes to transmute.

Why Look for a "Charge" after Saying the Spell Types?

Checking the spell types towards the end of the healing helps you determine whether all levels of your energy field are clear. This type of energy carries a "charge" or aggressive vibration that you are capable of sensing. When you are no longer detecting a charge, you can be sure that the negative influence has been eliminated, and the healing is complete.

Why End with Other Divine Tools?

Always conclude this healing with a large dose of Divine Energy. These powerful positive energies fill the space in your system where the negativity was held. Then use the Cutting Binding Ties Tool to cut the ties between you and everything that has been released. End with empowering yourself by closing and strengthening your aura. These steps bring your system back into connection with Divine Mother and your Infinite Self.

You Are More Powerful than These Issues

These issues occur rarely, and you may never use this Healing Tool. You are a Light Being working with Divine Mother and the Company of Heaven. There is nothing more powerful than that. When you hold enough Light, curses can't touch you. The limited intelligence that supports the issues named here is immature and misguided. Proceed with assurance that your Divine status enables you to send these negative energies into the Light, where they can transform and serve Divine Mother's Love.

Suggestions for Using Canceling Spells and Curses

If you have felt at any time that you are under a spell or a curse, free yourself by using this Canceling Spells Tool. This will make a huge difference in your life.

A friend told me that after he broke up with his girlfriend, she put a love spell on him to get him back. He felt very uncomfortable, and he used this tool to free himself and bring back his personal power.

If a divorce or other relationship becomes acrimonious, with nasty threats hurled from one partner to another, use the Canceling Spells Tool to completely dismantle the destructive energy set in motion by the negatively empowered words. Continue to shatter and break the energy until you feel the negativity has been completely neutralized. Then complete the Tool as instructed to empower the Light.

Light Exercise

This exercise intensifies Light in any area that you wish to transform. It could be in a relationship, legal situation, diseased part of your body, or anything else that needs to be healed and lifted for the highest good.

Start by Setting Your Intention

Make a statement about what you wish to transform. For example: "I am bringing Light into my relationship to transform it for the highest good for all concerned." Divine Intelligence will know how to create highest good. You don't have to worry about it or have an agenda about it with your individual will. Let Divine Will operate here.

Preparation

This exercise is an intention in the Wholeness of awareness. It's important to be settled and peaceful when you begin.

If you decide to use this exercise as part of a vibrational healing session, you will already be settled.

If using it outside a healing sequence, begin with the Softening Exercise to become centered and quiet. When you are settled, then begin.

First Stage:

> **Allow Light ...**
> **Allow more Light ...**
> **Allow more Light ...**
> **More Light ...**
> **More Light ...**
> **More Light ...**
> **Fill with Light ...**
> **Overflow with Light ...** (Keep allowing more Light until you feel it is time to shift.)

Second Stage:

> **Hold Light ...**
> **Hold ...**
> **Hold ...**
> **Hold ...**
> **Hold Light ...**

Soften, no strain, continue to Hold Light.

Hold ... Hold ... Hold Light ...

Hold ... (until you feel it is time to shift)

Third Stage:

> **Let go ...**
> **Let go ...**
> **Let go ...**
> **Let go and fall into the Infinite Source ...**
> **Keep letting go ...**

<u>Begin again</u> with the First Stage.

Repeat the three stages three times or more to completely saturate the situation with Light.

Conclusion:

> **Then let go ...**
> **Allow ...**
> **Be ...**
> **Trust ...**

Finish with:

> **Thank you Divine Mother, and so it is.**

About the Light Exercise

What Does the Light Exercise Do?

This exercise is a way to powerfully infuse Light into any situation for positive transformation. You will find that practicing it takes you deep into the Infinite Source while keeping your attention active. In other words, you are anchored in the Infinite Source while focusing Divine Light to transform yourself or situations in the world.

How Does It Work?

In this exercise, the focus of your consciousness activates the transformative power of Light in any object. Attention guides the flow of consciousness. You are focusing your attention and activating Light in something that you want to heal. It could be your body, a person, a relationship, or anything. Through the process of allowing more Light, holding Light, and letting go, the Light intensifies in the object of your focus. The creative power of Light then transforms the condition.

Where Does the Light Come From?

You are manifesting the Light from the Infinite Source with your intention. You say, "Allow Light," and the Light appears. You are creating it, calling it into form. You are a Divine Being in physical form. As a Divine Being, you have this ability.

Understanding the Three Steps

The Light Exercise gives you the ability to transform something with Light. The words are simple and minimal in order to let the vibration of Light take over.

In the first stage, you allow the flow of Light to stream in. You don't have to move the Light with your effort. Just the *intention* of "allowing" begins and continues the process.

Next, you "hold" Light, creating a container of consciousness in which the Light intensifies its power and increases its magnitude.

In the last stage, you "let go" naturally falling deeper into the Infinite Source.

"Letting go" means you are expanding your consciousness, collecting more fuel from Source to power up the activity of transformation.

Then you start again with "Allow Light …" By repeating this three-step process at least three times, you create a powerful infusion of Light.

When Do I Use It?

When there is a powerful issue that needs shifting, this exercise will flood it with Light to create change.

In a healing session, if there is persistent agitation or a stubborn block that resists release, this exercise works quickly to clear it.

Use it for big issues that come up, such as healing ingrained physical conditions, stubborn relationship problems, or troubling world issues. Any intransigent issue can be transformed in a positive way by this intense focus of Light.

This Tool can also effect supportive changes in sudden emergencies like accidents and other traumatic or stressful events.

Suggestions for Using the Light Exercise

Use this exercise to infuse your relationship with a powerful blast of Light at times when you and your partner are disconnected and can't communicate.

The Light Exercise can be used to break through partisan gridlock and create more cooperation. Even national and international problems respond to the consistent application of Light.

A friend was at a business conference when someone near her fell to the floor with a medical emergency. Everyone was startled and concerned. My friend felt an impulse to stand with her palms pointing towards the fallen person and do the Light Exercise until medical help arrived. Afterwards many people thanked her for what she did. They didn't know what was going on inside but sensed it was powerful and necessary. You can use the Light Exercise for supporting people in similar situations.

Divine Joy

Breathe into the heart and soften.

The power of Divine Joy is transforming my life now. I am filled with Divine Joy. I am embraced by Divine Joy.

The Joy of Divine Mother's Love is filling me now. I am receiving the Joy of Divine Mother's Presence within me now. I know that I am loved and cherished unconditionally. I experience the Joy of being held and cradled in Divine Mother's arms.

Divine Joy is my constant state. I am soaked and saturated with Divine Joy. Joy is always available to me as I live my everyday life. I am overjoyed by the beauty of the earth around me. My life is saturated with Joy in every moment. Divine Joy is an indelible part of me now. I am living a life of wonder and Joy.

Thank you Divine Mother, and so it is.

About Divine Joy

What Is Divine Joy?

Divine Joy is the Love of Divine Mother in tangible form. It is the rapture of the experience of Divine Mother's Love.

What Does It Do?

Divine Joy brings you into contact with Divine Mother's vibrant Love for the purpose of enjoying your life. When you are experiencing Joy, you are experiencing Divine Mother. Joy unites you with Divine Mother.

Everyone benefits when you are joyful. The vibration of Divine Joy supports health and healing in the body. The vibrancy of joy affects not only you but others as well. As you emanate joy, it lifts the whole atmosphere. When you are joyful, others catch the wave, literally a vibrational wave. Express your joy, it is contagious and you will lift many. It is a blessing for everyone.

When Do I Use It?

Use Divine Joy all the time. It's important to use it when you are sad or depressed to change your inner environment. It's important to use it when you are happy to increase your happiness. Use it when you or someone else is ill or when your home needs a vibrational lifting.

Divine Joy can be used anytime, anywhere, and will always have a positive influence.

Suggestions for Using Divine Joy

A colleague reported that she had been working for hours and was tired and depleted of energy. She read the Divine Joy Tool and it lifted her spirits, expanded her awareness, and focused her heart on the task at hand with renewed enthusiasm.

Whenever you want to feel the presence of Divine Mother, use the Divine Joy Tool to bring Her to you in a very personal and delightful way.

If you have been bothered by sadness and depression, regular use of this Tool can fill you with Divine Joy and help to change your experience of life.

Chapter 9

Healing on the Run

You can use Divine Mother's Healing Tools in quick abbreviated versions throughout a busy day. They will help dissolve negative energy and break through blocks you may encounter. You are becoming a Master of Energy, so you can apply these Tools and techniques to all situations in your life to make life smoother, easier, and more joyful.

The shortened Tools are quick fixes, and do not replace the deeper healing and long-term transformational effect gained by using the entire healing system. However, the quick healing methods below can smooth a rough incident and instantly bless those around you.

Some daily situations may aggravate deeper long-standing issues, and you will need a thorough Divine Mother Healing to dissolve them. Do this as soon as time allows to get the issue fully resolved.

1. Call on a Divine Being.

Say or think the name of any Divine Being, calling upon God in a personal form (Divine Mother, Mother Mary, Jesus Christ, Archangel Michael, or any other Great Being who recognizes they are Whole and One with God). This immediately connects you to this Divine Being for help and protection. This connection and assistance will be enough to shift the direction of the situation.

From Invocation of the Divine Beings

2. Breathe into the Heart.

Breathe into the heart and notice the whole chest area. Continue to breathe into whatever is tight or tense in the chest area until it dissolves and you experience peace.

From the Heart Exercise

3. Pour Divine Light into a Person or a Situation.

Say or think, "Divine Light is pouring into _____ [a person or situation]," and other phrases from the Divine Light Tool. Then imagine or visualize this happening. You can do this for people, events, conditions, or whenever there is tension, anger, fear, or other agitation. This fills the situation with Light.

From Divine Light

4. Bombs of Light

In any situation that is heavy, stuck, or negative, a quick way to bring Light into it is to burst or explode Light. This works effectively to "lighten" a situation. Imagine Light bursting or exploding in the negativity of a person, group, or world conflict. Exploding Light increases and expands Light.

From Divine Light

5. Say "Go!" to Discord and Negativity.

Say "Go" whenever sensing the energy of negativity around you or another person. State the command "Go! Go into the Light!" from the power of your God Self. You can say "Go" quietly inside if someone else is around.

From the Go Command

6. Break Grids of Untruth.

Inwardly, say "Break" several times and image the grids breaking whenever you notice yourself or someone else repeating a pattern of fear, anger, guilt, shame, or self-criticism. This is especially useful in family or business situations where old patterns repeat.

From the Break Command

7. Close Holes in Your Aura.

If you have been feeling fine and suddenly notice anger, heaviness, fatigue, or negativity, you may be experiencing the impact of other people's negative energies. Focus attention on closing holes in your auric field. Imagine or "see" holes closing around you. This will help you become self-contained and protected from discord in the environment.

From Closing Holes in Your Aura

8. Empower Your Aura.

Empowering your aura is important whenever you feel influenced by another person or the environment. Techniques to empower your aura are: place yourself in a globe of Light; see doors closing to negative people and situations; imagine your aura sparkling and bursting with Light; visualize Light flowing around you in a spiral from your feet to above your head.

From Aura Empowerment

9. Protect People or Property with Light.

If you are worried about someone's safety, see them surrounded with Light. Circle your home with Light. Place Archangel Michael all around the person or property, in front, back, above, below, to the left and right sides. Surround your vehicle with Light and Archangel Michael's presence while driving. Do this immediately if you almost have an accident or even the thought of an accident. Intend that the Light be strong, clear, and protective.

From Divine Light

10. Soften.

Soften whenever you find yourself tightening up, pulling back, or disconnecting. Softening helps you become bigger than the situation by expanding your energy through it, and connecting you to the bigger picture of what is going on. This expanded view can show you solutions and help you step out of the limitations of the problem.

From the Softening Exercise

11. Pour in Love.

Whenever you are disturbed, upset, or concerned about a person, relationship, condition, or world event, fill it with Divine Love. Say or think, "Divine Love is pouring into _____ [name the condition] now." Don't get caught in the negativity. You are not powerless. Pour Love into the situation. If you cannot do it yourself, ask Divine Mother or a favorite Divine Being to do it. This keeps you connected to Divine Energy rather than connected to the presenting negativity.

From Divine Love

12. Cut Binding Ties.

When you can't get out of recurring thoughts, emotions, or images, it helps to quickly use the Cutting Binding Ties Tool. Ask Divine Mother or Archangel Michael to cut binding ties between you and the issue. "See" or "feel" the ties being cut layer by layer until you notice relief. Cut binding ties between you and people that bother or have hurt you. Cut the ties between you and any obsessive thoughts.

From Cutting Binding Ties

13. Stop Self-Criticism.

Whenever you catch yourself thinking something like "That was a dumb thing to do … I'm hopeless … I'm an idiot," immediately stop and say good things about yourself, like "I am okay …

I can handle this … I am a good person … I am doing fine … I know what I'm doing … I'm smart." Say the opposite of the insult you just gave yourself. Then drop it and move on.

From the Self-Love Exercise

Examples of Using Healing on the Run

If you see a parent being angry and harsh with a child, surround them with Light and break grids of anger and distress.

When driving, if you draw negativity from another driver, say "Go, Go, Go into the Light" to clear the negative energy around them and yourself. Then fill them with Divine Light.

When you are with someone who is angry and upset, breathe into your heart and center yourself in your heart so that you are not drawn into their disturbance. By staying centered in your heart, you can be of more help.

When your children are arguing with each other, pour in Divine Light and silently say "Go, Go, Go into the Light" to the negativity. Then help them resolve their differences.

When your toddler is climbing to the top of the jungle-gym or approaching some possible danger, circle him or her with Light until you can get near enough to ensure their safety.

Any time you have fear for your children's safety when they are not with you, circle them with Light and call upon a Divine Being to stand with them.

When you are watching the news and there are people suffering, pour in Divine Light and breathe into your heart.

When you can't get negative thoughts out of your mind, use the Go Command to dissolve them in the Light.

When you are obsessing over a relationship problem, cut binding ties with the person and pour Divine Love into the relationship.

If you have a nightmare, cut ties with it and say "Go, Go, Go into the Light" to the energy of fear.

If a policeman stops you for speeding, call on a Divine Being to surround him, you, and your car with Light. You may not even get a ticket!

Every time you drive, surround your car with Light and place Archangel Michael, the Protector Angel, all around it.

During any argument, breathe into your heart and call on a Divine Being.

When you are going to an appointment, fill the appointment with Light before you get there.

When you are impatient with your children or your spouse and feel yourself getting angry, start breathing into your heart to help you stay calm.

Use the Break Command in your office any time your team needs to break out of old thinking patterns and embrace fresh new ideas.

Pour in Divine Love as you are traveling to visit your family to keep the petty annoyances and irritations that family members often have with each other to a minimum. While you are there, if anything comes up, start silently pouring in Divine Love. This will smooth out family issues and allow all of you to have a wonderful time together.

If you find yourself in a congested or agitated environment, perhaps at an airport or concert, close holes in your aura. It will help you to maintain your inner integrity and feeling of safety.

Part Three

Start Healing

Chapter 10

Four Ways to Use the Tools

Here in Part Three of this book, you have easy access for using Divine Mother's Tools for a healing. The following are four ways you may choose to work with these powerful Healing Tools to help you with your life challenges and connect you to Divine Mother:

1. Full Session
2. Short Session
3. Mini-Session
4. Healing on the Run

Select the one you would like to use. The Full Session will always give you the most thorough healing. When pressed for time, use the Short Session or Mini-Session. Whichever one you decide upon, Divine Mother will work with you to empower you with her energy and protection. The fourth option, "Healing on the Run," gives you brief versions of the Tools that you can use quickly in daily activity anytime a challenge arises.

If you have any questions about a Healing Tool, what it does or how to use it, refer to the "About" section for that Tool. (If you need help locating a particular "About," all of the Tools are listed in the Table of Contents under Chapters 7 and 8. Each Tool's explanation immediately follows the text for that Tool.)

In every case, you are aligning with Divine Mother, filling with Her Energy, and dissolving the discord in your system.

Recommended Sequences

Full Session Sequence - *pg. 133*

Heart Exercise – Short Form
Invocation of the Divine Beings
Softening Exercise
Divine Light
Closing Holes in Your Aura
First Go Command
Releasing Agreements
Calling Back Parts
Deep Go Command
Break Command
Divine Nectar
Divine Love
Divine Truth
Ascending Light
Cutting Binding Ties
Divine Grace
Closing a Divine Mother Healing Session

Short Session Sequence - *pg. 161*

Heart Exercise – Short Form
Invocation of the Divine Beings
Softening Exercise
Divine Light
Closing Holes in Your Aura
First Go Command
Break Command
Divine Nectar
Divine Love
Cutting Binding Ties
Closing a Divine Mother Healing Session

Mini-Session Sequence - *pg. 181*

Heart Exercise – Mini-Form
Invoke Divine Mother
Closing Holes in Your Aura
First Go Command
Ascending Light

Healing on the Run - *pg. 205*

Use of a Tool in abbreviated form
outside of a session sequence.

Specialized Healing Tools - *pg. 189*

Self-Love Exercise
Creating the Flow of Love
Heart Exercise – Long Form
Spinning Ascending Light
Aura Empowerment
Canceling Spells and Curses
The Light Exercise
Divine Joy

Chapter 11

Full Session

Heart Exercise – Short Form

To start a Divine Mother healing session:

Breathe into the heart center, not just the heart organ, but the whole chest area. Breathe as if the breath is coming through the front of the chest into the heart and soften in the heart to receive the breath. Allow the heart to open, like a flower opening its petals, to receive the warm, soft breath.

If you can't keep your attention in the heart, take many strong, deep breaths (10 to 15) into the chest area. The deep breaths quiet mental activity and then you can focus attention on the heart.

The breath carries life energy. Soften in the heart as your receive the breath. Notice the flow of breath moving into the heart center.

Continue to put your attention on the heart center, which is the whole chest area, not just the heart organ. Notice if there is any tightness or discomfort there. If there is, breathe into it, allowing the breath to move through it, opening it up, and moving the flow of breath through the discomfort.

Practice the Heart Exercise for a minute or two before beginning the Invocation. This dissolves blockages and connects you to your heart. Keep breathing into the heart throughout the Invocation as you unite with Divine Mother and the Great Beings of the universe. Then begin the healing sequence.

Doing the Heart Exercise and then going right into the Invocation helps you connect to Divine Mother, who is actually conducting the healing. This process is designed to move you out of your small self and settle you into your heart.

Invocation of the Divine Beings

Start by saying:

I am Whole. I am One with God. I am One in the Infinite Wholeness of all that is. I call upon Almighty Mother-Father God and all of the beautiful expressions of Divine Love who know and live the Wholeness of Divine Truth.

I call upon these Great Divine Beings now ...

Here, name those Great Beings who recognize their Wholeness and Oneness with God. Below is a list of some of the Divine Ones the author calls upon. It is not necessary to invite all of them. You may call upon the names below or only those who are familiar to you. Or just call upon Divine Mother or Mother-Father God.

I call upon the presence of Divine Mother in Her many aspects. I call upon Mother Mary (Christian), **Shekhina** (Jewish), **the Divine Presence of Fatima** (Islam), **Mother Lakshmi, Saraswati, Durga, Kali, Parvati** (Hindu). **I invite Tara and Quan Yin** (Buddhist), **Amaterasu** (Shinto), **White Buffalo Calf Woman** (Native American). I call upon **Gaia, Mother Earth, and Prakriti, Mother Nature. I invite all the expressions of Divine Mother from the world's traditions of Truth.**

I invite those Great Beings and Master Teachers around whom many of the world's spiritual traditions have grown. I call upon Jesus Christ and the Holy Spirit (Christian), **Abraham and Moses** (Jewish), **the Divine Presence of Mohammed** (Islam), **Lord Buddha** (Buddhist), **Lao Tzu** (Taoist), **Lord Krishna, Lord Ram, Lord Vishnu, Lord Shiva, Lord Brahma** (Hindu).

I call upon the Archangels: Archangels Michael, Gabriel, Raphael, Uriel, Zadkiel, Chamuel, Jophiel, Metatron, and all Archangels. (You may wish to add others.)

I invite the Ascended Masters: Babaji, Sananda, Serapis Bey, Saint Germain, Brother Francis of Assisi, Lady Nada, and all the Ascended Masters. (You may wish to add others.)

I invite the Gurus (Spiritual Teachers). (Name those fully enlightened Gurus who are significant in your life.)

Continue with:

There is a protective sphere of Holy Light surrounding me now, creating a sacred space. Archangel Michael and his legions of angels guard and protect this sacred space, so that only the energies of the Archangels, Ascended Masters, and Beings of Light holding the Wholeness of Divine Truth may enter this space. Archangel Michael stands in front of me, behind me, to the right of me, to the left of me, above me, and below me. I am safe and protected within this sacred sphere of Holy Light.

The loving, liquid, golden, healing substance of Divine Love is continually pouring into me throughout this healing session, allowing all the healing, lifting, and energy shifting to be smooth, comfortable, and complete.

I invite these Great Divine Beings to be present here now, to lift and heal me.

If there is a specific issue say:

Please heal the issue of _____

Name whatever you want to have healed. If there is not a specific issue at this time, continue with the healing sequence and know that the healing will be for your highest good in all areas.

Thank you Divine Mother, and so it is.

Softening Exercise

This exercise uses the power of attention and intention. The process is to move the attention to a specific place with the intention to soften there.

Softening is a relaxing or letting go of rigid boundaries. You are putting your attention on a specific place and then softening the boundaries of that place, letting your awareness flow beyond the boundaries.

Read the steps of the exercise, practicing it while you read it. Let your attention go to the area of the body named and soften there. The intent to soften is enough; don't try to make it happen.

Go slowly and pause each time you soften.

Here is the process:

> Soften in the heart …
> Soften in the heart center, not just the heart organ, but the whole chest area.
> Move your attention to the throat, soften in the throat …
> Soften the boundaries of the throat.
> Move your attention to the brow, which includes the brow area and the place between the eyebrows, often called the third eye. The attention is on the brow area.
> Soften in the brow/third eye …
> Soften at the top of the head, the crown …
> Soften at the base of the spine in the same way as you have been doing in the other energy centers.
> Soften in the pelvic area, the area below the navel, letting go in the pelvic area.
> Soften in the navel …
> Soften in the solar plexus, the diaphragm area above the navel.
> Soften again in the heart …

Repeat the above sequence at least three more times, ending by softening in the heart. Then continue with the following sequence:

> Soften in the cells.
> Soften in the brain, letting the brain melt like butter on a hot day.
> Soften in the whole body.
> Soften in the space around the body, the auric field.
> Soften in the navel.
> Soften in the heart.

Finish by inwardly saying:

> **I am Whole and One with All That Is.**
> **Thank you Divine Mother, and so it is.**

Divine Light

Soften in the heart.

Pause for a moment after every sentence, and read slowly. Repeat any of these paragraphs more than once if desired.

> **Divine Light is pouring into me now. Divine Light is filling my energy field on every level. Divine Light is increasing within me now. I am receiving more and more Divine Light, moment by moment. Divine Light is healing every limitation within my energy system and opening me to Wholeness now.**

Pause and continue reading slowly.

> **Divine Light is releasing all discord within my system now and opening me to more Divine Light. Divine Light is flooding my energy system now. I accept Divine Light within me now. I know that Divine Light is increasing its presence within my system and illuminating my entire energy field. The most refined, sublime quality of Light in creation is opening in my energy system and lifting my energy field into resonance with Sacred Light vibration.**

> **Divine Light is healing me now. This Sacred Light is lifting, opening, cleansing, and healing my entire system, and allowing the presence of Light to increase within me now. Divine Light is filling every organ, tissue, cell, atom, and particle of my body. Divine Light continues filling me and healing my entire energy field. I am inundated, saturated, permeated, and penetrated with Divine Light.**

Pause and continue to read slowly.

> **Divine Light is emerging from Source and overflowing on every level of my energy field, nourishing my system with more Divine Light. I am receiving wave after wave of Light. I am filled with Light. More Divine Light is awakening in my entire system and releasing all that is not Whole.**

> **The Wholeness of Divine Light fills me now. All energies of limitation and lack are dissolving as Divine Light vibrates throughout my energy field. I am held in Divine Light. I am bathed in Divine Light. I am healed in Divine Light. I am lifted, opened, cleansed, and freed in Divine Light.**

> **Thank you Divine Mother, and so it is.**

Closing Holes in Your Aura

I call upon Divine Mother and Archangel Michael to close all doors, openings, holes, portals, and pathways anywhere in my multi-leveled energy system to all limited (*those that limit your Wholeness*) **planes, domains, dimensions, spheres, realms, and locations anywhere in creation.**

I command in the name of Divine Mother that all doors, openings, holes, portals, and pathways anywhere in my multi-leveled energy system are now closed and sealed to the following levels:

Go through the list one at a time and after naming each limited level say, **"Close!"** and see doors slam throughout all levels of your energy field. Then see, know, or feel the doors are closed and sealed.

> **I close doors to the astral plane ... CLOSE!** (Includes disembodied earthbound spirits)
>
> **I close doors to the limited extra-terrestrial entities ... CLOSE!**
>
> **I close doors to the inter-dimensional entities ... CLOSE!** (Other subtle life forms)
>
> **I close doors to false gods ... CLOSE!** (Anything you make more powerful than your Infinite Self)
>
> **I close doors to lost souls ... CLOSE!** (Beings who have lost their evolutionary path)
>
> **I close doors to negative thought forms ... CLOSE!**
>
> **I close doors to all dense, low-frequency beings ... CLOSE!**
>
> **I close doors to the fear and negativity in the world consciousness ... CLOSE!**
>
> **I close doors to all unknown limited beings ... CLOSE!**

Repeat from the authority of your Divine Self:

> **These doors, openings, holes, portals, and pathways are now closed and sealed, in the name and through the power of Divine Mother, in the name and through the power of Archangel Michael.**

Again, image doors closing and sealing all around you. Focused attention on the holes closing is important.

Then say:

> **Any energetic configurations or attracting mechanisms around these now closed holes and openings are dismantled, broken, dissolved, and released.**

I am now opening into my authentic Self and moving through my individual life with Grace, Power, and Divine Integrity.

See or feel or know that a strong shield of protective Light is all around you, very vibrant and powerful.

End by saying:

I am aligned with Truth. I am Whole.
Thank you Divine Mother, and so it is.

First Go Command

This Tool clears the discord and blockages that have accumulated in the subtle fields of your energy system and are compromising the full expression of your True Self. Later in the healing session, the Deep Go Command Tool will clear blockages at even deeper levels.

Breathe into the heart. Say:

> **I call upon Divine Mother and all the Divine Beings to release and clear all discordant energies, blockages, and confusion from the following levels of my system.**

First, clear the <u>emotional level</u>.

Say lovingly but firmly from your Divine Authority, not from your small self:

> **I now address all blockages and discord at the emotional level of my energy field. Go into the Light. Go … Go … Go … Go into the Light …**

As needed, repeat:

> **Go into the Light. Go … Go … Go … Go into the Light … Go … Go … Go … Go into the Light. In the name of God, I command you to go into the Light now.**

Continue repeating **"Go"** until you notice a shift, like a sense of expansion, a deep breath, or a settling indicating there has been a release.

You are clearing layers of your emotional system. By repeating **"Go into the Light"** over and over, you clear deeper and deeper layers. Keep repeating **"Go"** until you feel clear and complete at each level.

As you proceed, alternate saying **"Go"** with filling the level with Diving Light. Say:

> **Divine Light is filling the emotional level, Divine Light is pouring into the emotional level, Divine Light is saturating the emotional level, more and more Divine Light fills the emotional level.**

Then return to saying **"Go, Go into the Light …"** until you sense that level is clear and complete.

Next, clear the <u>mental level</u>. Say:

I now address all blockages and discord at the mental level of my energy field. Go into the Light. Go, Go, Go …

At every level, follow the same instructions for clearing as stated above.

Now clear the <u>etheric level</u>. Say:

I now address all blockages and discord at the etheric level of my energy field. Go into the Light. Go, Go, Go …

Follow instructions as stated above.

Clear the <u>physical level</u>. Say:

I now address all blockages and discord at the physical level of my energy field. Go into the Light. Go, Go, Go …

Follow instructions as stated above.

Clear the <u>astral level</u>. Say:

I now address all blockages and discord at the astral level of my energy field Go into the Light. Go, Go, Go …

Follow instructions as stated above.

Clear the <u>causal level</u>. Say:

I now address all blockages and discord at the causal level of my energy field. Go into the Light. Go, Go, Go …

Follow instructions as stated above.

Clear the <u>celestial level</u>. Say:

I now address all blockages and discord at the celestial level of my energy field. Go into the Light. Go, Go, Go …

Follow instructions as stated above.

Clear the level of <u>Pure Spirit</u>. Pure Spirit is always clear. Here, we clear any mental, emotional, and spiritual misconceptions which limit the experience of this level. Say:

I now address all blockages and discord at the level of Pure Spirit. Go into the Light. Go, Go, Go …

Follow instructions as stated above.

Finally, clear the <u>Avenue of Awareness</u>, which governs the way life is perceived. Say:

I now address all blockages and discord in the Avenue of Awareness. Go into the Light. Go, Go, Go …

Follow instructions as stated above.

Then conclude by saying:

All limited energies, entities, and negative programs are now released and let go on every level of my energy system. All doors, openings, holes, portals, or pathways to these areas are now closed and sealed.

See, know, and feel your aura is strong and powerful.

Then say:

I am now opening into the Wholeness of my Authentic Self, and it is flowing through my individual life with Grace, Power, and Divine Integrity.

Thank you Divine Mother, and so it is.

Releasing Agreements

Breathe into the heart.

> **I call upon Divine Mother and Archangel Michael to cancel, release, and dissolve all contracts, agreements, vows, commitments, trades, or exchanges that I may have made in this lifetime or any other that are blocking or limiting my recognition and full expression of who I am now.**

> **These contracts, agreements, vows, commitments, trades, and exchanges are now canceled, released, dissolved, let go, and made null and void, in the name and through the power of Divine Mother, in the name and through the power of Archangel Michael.**

Image or "feel" the dissolution of the agreements, or "see" the contract breaking.

> **All frameworks, structures, circuitry, and grids that have developed as a result of these now canceled contracts and conditions are dissolved, collapsed, broken, released, and let go on every level of my energy field.**

Image the frameworks, etc., breaking or dissolving as you say:

> **Break, Break, Break …**

Continue to repeat **"Break,"** energetically breaking the contracts and agreements until the energy is light and free. This can take several minutes.

> **These frameworks and structures are now completely dissolved, and I am free.**

End by saying:

> **I am filled with Divine Love.**
> **I am aligned with Divine Truth.**
> **I am Whole.**
> **Thank you Divine Mother, and so it is.**

Calling Back Parts

Breathe into the heart.

Say inwardly or out loud:

> **In the name of Divine Mother, I call back all parts of myself that have been separated, isolated, lost, given away, taken, or forgotten. I call these parts back into the Wholeness of my heart now.**

Breathe into the heart center as if the breath is pulling all parts and pieces of yourself back into the Wholeness of your heart.

This may be repeated until you feel you are completely back.

Next say:

> **I call back all parts of myself that have been left behind in former jobs, challenges, people, activities, projects, and relationships. I call these parts back into the Wholeness of my heart.**

Breathe into the heart center as if the breath is pulling all parts and pieces of yourself back into the Wholeness of your heart.

Next say:

> **I call back all my power that I have given away. I call back all the parts of myself that I have hidden.**

Breathe into the heart center as if the breath is pulling all parts and pieces of yourself back into the Wholeness of your heart.

Repeat inwardly or out loud:

> **I call back these parts of myself into the Wholeness of my heart and I claim my Wholeness now.**

Breathe again into the heart, pulling yourself back into the Wholeness of your heart.

Optional:

> You can call yourself back from specific issues as needed.
> **I call myself back from _____** [name the specific issue].

Examples: **I draw myself back from my relationship with** _____ [name], **my** _____ [family member], **my job at** _____, **the abuse from** _____ [name].

Then repeat:

> **I call back all parts of myself into the Wholeness of my heart and I claim my Whole Self now.**

Any of these may be repeated several times if they are particularly relevant to your life experience.

End with:

> **I welcome all parts of myself back into the Wholeness of my heart now.**
> **I know that I am Whole and One with All That Is.**
> **Thank you Divine Mother, and so it is.**

Deep Go Command

After clearing the levels of your energy field earlier in the sequence with the First Go Command, deeper blocks and discord that were previously hidden are often revealed. As you move through the healing sequence, the Deep Go Command is now enlisted.

Breathe into the heart as you read the Tool. Speak from your Divine Self, not your small ego, using the power of your Divine Self to send these constricting energies into the Light.

I am Whole and One with All That Is. I am aligned with Divine Truth. In the name of Truth, in the name of Love, I call upon Divine Mother to release all limited energies, entities, and negative programs from my system now.

I say to these limitations and blockages:

"You must go. Divine Mother is here to take you into the Light. Look for the Light. Look for Divine Mother. Go into the Light and the Love and the Heart of Divine Mother."

Take two or three more breaths into your heart and say to the blockages:

Go into the Light!

Continue taking deep breaths into the heart and say the word **"Go!"** out loud. Repeat the command:

Go into the Light!

Remember to say this out loud, lovingly but firmly from your Divine Authority, not from your small self.

Optional: To strengthen the command, follow the word **"Go"** by blowing out the breath, as if blowing the limitations away.

Repeat:

Go into the Light ... Go ... Go ... Go... Go into the Light ... Go ... Go ... Go ... Go into the Light ... In the name of God, I command you to go into the Light now. Go ... Go ...

Optional: Alternate statements to use at your discretion during the process.

I am Infinite and Whole. I command you in the name of my Infinite Self to leave my energy system now. Go into the Light.

I give you permission to go into the Light. Go ...

I give myself permission to let go.

As your voice settles and becomes more quiet, continue repeating **"Go into the Light"** inwardly to clear the limited energies at the more subtle levels of your system. Keep softening and know that the healing is being done by Divine Mother, not your individuality.

Keep repeating **"Go"** until you feel centered, expansive, light, and clear. This can take a few minutes or longer, until you feel complete. Then conclude by saying:

I am Whole. I am aligned with Truth.
Thank you Divine Mother, and so it is.

Break Command

Breathe into the heart and center in your Divine Self, which is in the heart. Continue breathing into the heart and say the following words:

I call upon Divine Mother, Archangel Michael, and all the Divine Beings to break, shatter, and dissolve all old patterns, grids, frameworks, structures, and multidimensional matrices that are limiting me or holding negative energies in my system. These structures are now broken, shattered, cracked up, dissolved, released, and completely let go throughout my multidimensional energy system.

Then take some deep breaths through the heart and chest to activate the life force for healing and transforming your system.

Say the word **"Break!"** out loud (silently if other people not involved in the healing are nearby) and image these structures breaking, shattering, and dissolving. Your imaging tells the energy what to do.

Repeat the word "**Break**!" lovingly but firmly from your Divine Authority, not from your small self.

Say **"Break! Break! Break ..."** many times as deeper layers of your system are cleared of the old structures, while continuously imaging the structures breaking and collapsing.

As you say **"Break,"** your voice may soften as you reach the deeper levels of your system. At some point, it will be appropriate to say **"Break"** inwardly. Keep repeating **"Break,"** imaging and feeling the structures dismantling at deeper, more subtle levels. Soften and let go as you break these structures.

In addition to saying **"Break, Break,"** you can use the words, **"Shatter," "Burst," "Smash," "Dissolve," "Melt," "Collapse,"** or other words commanding the dissolution of the old stuck vibrational patterns and structures.

Remember to keep softening and letting go, knowing that the Divine power is doing the breaking, not your individual will.

Notice your energy as you do this and continue until you have a sense of new freedom and expansion in your energy field.

End with:

These old grids, frameworks, and structures are now completely broken, shattered, and dissolved and I am Whole. I am aligned with Truth.

Thank you Divine Mother, and so it is.

Finish by bringing in the Divine Nectar, the liquid Love, to nourish your system and fill the space, now that these grids of untruth are gone. It is the next Tool in the sequence.

Divine Nectar

Breathe into the heart. Soften and let go of any tension. Allow the heart to expand.

Say:

> I am One in the Wholeness of all that is. I am receiving the Love of Divine Mother soaking into me as a nectar-like substance, the pure essence of Divine Love.
>
> I am filling with Divine Nectar now. This Divine Nectar, the essence of Divine Love, is healing me. I am receiving this Liquid Love on every level of my entire energy field. Divine Nectar is pouring into me. I am bathed in Divine Nectar. I am filled with Divine Nectar. I am healed by Divine Nectar.
>
> Liquid Love is healing me as it flows through my system. I am soaking in the sacred Nectar. My heart is being soothed by Liquid Love. The loving flow of Divine Nectar is filling my body, healing every cell, every organ, and every system. My head is filling with Divine Nectar, calming my thoughts, soothing my brain, soaking into my cells. I am filled with Liquid Love.

(Pause and notice the Divine Nectar. Stay soft and centered in the Divine Self in your heart while saying these words.)

> I am letting go of harmful thoughts. I am healing my thinking process. I am opening to Divine Nectar in my head and in my heart. The Nectar is continuing to flood my body. I am healing in this essence of Divine Mother's Love. Divine Nectar is filling me with Liquid Love, and my system is healing the sadness, pain, and suffering.
>
> I am allowing Divine Nectar to increase within me now. I am filling with this Nectar of Love. I am releasing all fear and trusting Divine Nectar to heal everything that is afraid. The waves of Liquid Love are flowing into me, saturating me with their loving caress. I am receiving Divine Nectar.
>
> I open to the flowing Nectar and allow its waves of Love to fill my heart, my body, my mind, and my energy field. I accept Divine Nectar within me now.

Repeat this as often as desired to enrich your system with the healing, soothing presence of Divine Nectar.

> **Thank you Divine Mother, and so it is.**

Divine Love

Soften in the heart.

Pause for a moment after every sentence, and read slowly. Repeat any of these paragraphs more than once if desired.

> **Divine Love is pouring into me now. I am receiving Divine Love on every level of my existence. I am opening to allow Divine Love to fill me and overflow in my life now.**

> **I accept Divine Love within me now. I am inundated, saturated, permeated, and penetrated with Divine Love. Divine Love fills me again and again on deeper and deeper levels of my existence.**

Have a gentle awareness of Divine Love.

Read slowly and pause between each sentence.

> **I am healing in Divine Love. The Love of Divine Mother is pouring into every atom, cell, organ, and system of my entire physical body. I am flooded with Divine Love, bathed in Divine Love, cleansed by Divine Love.**

> **I open and accept Divine Love within me now on every level of my life expression.**

> **The lively, dynamic energy of Divine Love is cleansing, dissolving, and transmuting all energies of lack and limitation within my energy system. I am opening to the presence of more and more life energy of Divine Love. The vital life energy of Divine Love is transmuting all energies of discord within me now. Radiant, vibrant Divine Love is erasing all error conditioning, all error patterning, all limited belief systems, and all limiting self-concepts.**

> **Divine Love is opening in the deepest areas of my energy field. The oldest, most lost, forgotten, ignored areas of my system are receiving Divine Love. Divine Love is welling up from deep within, dissolving all blocked energy within my energy field. More and more Divine Love is opening within me now. Old ancestral patterning is releasing now. All old frequencies, from this life or any other, this dimension or any other, are releasing now. Old frequencies, old conditioning, old energies from the past are letting go, releasing, and lifting.**

Notice and allow. Keep letting go to allow the Divine Love.

Read slowly and pause between each sentence.

Divine Love is radiant within me now. Divine Love is increasing its presence within my energy field. The life energy of Divine Love is pulsating within my energy system now, in unison with the heartbeat of the Creator. I am radiant with Divine Love.

I am One with the fullness of Divine Mother's Love.

I am moving in the Wholeness of Divine Love as Divine Love creates more and more Love within me now.

Thank you Divine Mother, and so it is.

Divine Truth

Soften in the heart.

Pause for a moment after every sentence, and read slowly.

I am Whole and One with All That Is.

I accept the Divine Truth of my Infinite Wholeness now.

Wholeness of Divine Truth is awakening in my energy field. Wholeness of Divine Truth is filling me now. Wholeness of Divine Truth is opening throughout my energy system on every level of my life expression. Divine Truth knows only Oneness and is establishing the Truth of Oneness throughout my energy system now.

All untruth is letting go as Divine Truth fills my energy field with the Truth that I am Whole and One with God. Divine Truth is building the Presence of Truth in my energy system. This Presence of Truth is expanding and increasing Divine Truth throughout my physical and subtle fields.

I accept Divine Truth within me now on every level of my life expression.

All untruth anywhere in my multidimensional energy system is releasing, letting go, and changing into Truth. Divine Truth is Whole and complete within my energy system. I am healed by Truth. Truth allows Infinite Wholeness to be fully present within my energy system. Divine Truth carries wisdom and fills me with the Wisdom of Oneness now.

Truth is opening me into Wholeness again and again, freeing every place, point, and space in my energy field to vibrate Divine Truth. The untruth is collapsing now. Divine Truth is building a home of Truth within me, and I am healing in Wholeness of Divine Truth. Divine Truth is established within me now.

I accept the Divine Truth of my Infinite Wholeness now.

Finish with:

Thank you Divine Mother, and so it is.

Ascending Light

Breathe into the heart.

Ascending Light is lifting me now. Ascending Light is pouring into my energy system. Ascending Light is moving throughout my multi-leveled energy field. Ascending Light is resonating on every level of my system, opening me to more Ascending Light. I accept Ascending Light within me now, in every aspect of my life expression.

I am radiant with Ascending Light and Ascending Light is increasing its presence within me moment by moment. I am being transformed in Ascending Light so that I may become all that I am capable of becoming.

Ascending Light is lifting and clearing all ancestral patterning within my energy system. Ascending Light is freeing my system from all limiting energies and frequencies. I allow Ascending Light to free me now.

Ascending Light is filling my cells. It is healing my cells as they vibrate with Ascending Light. More and more Ascending Light is saturating my cells now.

Breathe into the heart. Have the intention to soften and allow the Ascending Light.

Ascending Light is entering my DNA. Ascending Light is freeing my DNA and restructuring it in Divine Truth. My DNA is overflowing with Ascending Light. I am being lifted, opened, cleansed, and healed in Ascending Light. I am filling with Ascending Light. I am accepting Ascending Light, and it is transforming me now. I allow Ascending Light to fill me now.

I am lifted, opened, cleansed, and freed in Ascending Light now.

I am Whole. I am One with All That Is. I am filled with Ascending Light.

You can repeat this as often as you like to raise your vibration with Ascending Light.

Thank you Divine Mother, and so it is.

Cutting Binding Ties

Breathe into the heart.

> **I ask Divine Mother and Archangel Michael with his Blue Flame Sword of Truth to lovingly cut all binding ties, hooks, threads, cords, attachments, and any other kind of tie that may be limiting me in any way.**

> **These ties are now cut between myself and _____ [name].** (Name specific persons, places, events, situations, or conditions where you have felt limited, bound, or attached in any way. If you are completing a full healing sequence, cut ties between yourself and everything that has been released during the healing session.)

Then say:

> **These binding ties, hooks, threads, cords, and attachments are now lovingly cut by Archangel Michael and his Blue Flame Sword of Truth. They are completely and thoroughly cut, lifted, healed, removed, dissolved, and released from every level of my multi-leveled energy field.**

Next say:

> **I ask Divine Mother and Archangel Michael to release all these ties and attachments from me now, layer, by layer, by layer.**

> **I allow these binding ties and attachments to be let go and transmuted into Light by Divine Mother now, layer, by layer, by layer.**

> **These ties are lovingly cut layer, by layer, by layer, by layer, by layer, by layer, by layer throughout my entire vibrational field.**

Image the ties being cut.

> **Even the subtlest ties are cut, lifted, healed, released, and dissolved layer, by layer, by layer, by layer.**

Repeat:

> **They are cut layer, by layer, by layer, by layer …**

… until you sense the release is complete. The repetition is important because you are cutting ties through every level of your multi-leveled energy system.

Then say:

I am free.

Finish with:

I know that I am Whole and One with All That Is.
Thank you Divine Mother, and so it is.

Divine Grace

Breathe into the heart.

The Wholeness of Divine Grace is completely filling my energy field now. Divine Grace is pouring into my energy field now, filling every place in my multi-leveled energy system with the presence of Divine Grace. Divine Grace is opening more Grace in my energy system, completely immersing me in the presence of Divine Grace.

I accept Divine Grace within me now on every level of my life expression.

Divine Grace is permeating, penetrating, and saturating my energy field with the Holy Presence of Divine Grace. Divine Grace is opening within every particle, atom, molecule, cell, point, place, and space within my entire energy field now.

More and more Wholeness of Divine Grace is filling me again and again. Wholeness of Divine Grace is pouring more Divine Grace into me now. I am lifted, opened, cleansed, and freed in the Wholeness of Divine Grace.

Divine Grace is opening again and again into me and into all areas of my life and gracing my entire energy field.

Divine Grace is bathing me on all levels of my life expression. Divine Grace is renewing and sustaining me in a life blessed with Divine Grace.

I am living in Divine Grace as I move through my life. I am lifted, opened, cleansed, and freed in Divine Grace.

Divine Grace is opening again and again within me now and gracing my entire existence. My life is now operating under the law of Divine Grace. I am now opening in Wholeness, moving in Grace, opening in Wholeness, moving in Grace.

Thank you Divine Mother, and so it is.

Closing a Divine Mother Healing Session

Breathe into your heart and say:

> **Thank you, Divine Mother and all the Beings of Wholeness, for the purification and alignment with Truth that I have received from you today.**

> **My heart is open and receiving your Divine Presence. I am moving with you through this day.**

> **The Love that you have for me is now resonating throughout my body, mind, and heart as I conduct my life in alignment with Divine Truth.**

> **I now allow Divine Love to flow into my physical body as I become active and engaged with the environment.**

Begin to gently move and stretch, slowly bringing the body from a resting state into activity.

> **I come into activity balanced and integrated with my physical surroundings.**

> **I know that Divine Mother is with me and that all is well.**

Say the following affirmations, speaking with confidence, knowing that it is so:

> **I am alert. I am clear. I am balanced within myself and with my outer environment.**

> **I am Whole. I am One with All That Is. I am divinely protected by Divine Mother's Love.**

> **I close all doors, openings, and holes in my energy field to the limited planes of existence now.**

> **I close to the astral plane** (pause a moment and say, "Close"); **to the limited extra-terrestrial regions, "Close"; to the inter-dimensional realms, "Close"; to the lost souls, "Close"; to the false gods, "Close"; to the negative thought forms, "Close"; to the heavy, dense energy beings, "Close"; and to the race-mind consciousness of Mother Earth, "Close." All doors, openings, holes to these regions are now closed and sealed in the name and through the power of Divine Mother.**

Image doors closing around you.

Then say:

My aura and body of light are radiant with Divine Presence.

Pause for a moment here to fill the aura with the Light. Sense, feel, know, image, and intend that your auric field, for about ten feet all around you, is brilliant with Light, sparkling with Light, glowing with Light, empowered and vibrant with Divine Light.

Then say:

I am aligned with Truth.
I am Whole.

End with three grounding breaths:

Take a deep breath into your body, bringing all of the Divine Love, Light, Truth, and Grace to fill your physical body, and then as you exhale, connect with Mother Earth by sending the energy into Mother Earth beneath your feet. Again, take another deep breath, bringing the Divine Energy into your body and exhale into Mother Earth. Then take one more breath, filling the physical body with Divine Energy, and as you exhale, ground yourself on Mother Earth.

Now say:

I am now moving through my life with Grace, Power, and Divine Integrity.
Thank you Divine Mother, and so it is.

Take any additional time you need to stretch, open your eyes slowly, and integrate with the environment.

Chapter 12

Short Session

Heart Exercise – Short Form

To start a Divine Mother healing session:

Breathe into the heart center, not just the heart organ, but the whole chest area. Breathe as if the breath is coming through the front of the chest into the heart and soften in the heart to receive the breath. Allow the heart to open, like a flower opening its petals, to receive the warm, soft breath.

If you can't keep your attention in the heart, take many strong, deep breaths (10 to 15) into the chest area. The deep breaths quiet mental activity and then you can focus attention on the heart.

The breath carries life energy. Soften in the heart as your receive the breath. Notice the flow of breath moving into the heart center.

Continue to put your attention on the heart center, which is the whole chest area, not just the heart organ. Notice if there is any tightness or discomfort there. If there is, breathe into it, allowing the breath to move through it, opening it up, and moving the flow of breath through the discomfort.

Practice the Heart Exercise for a minute or two before beginning the Invocation. This dissolves blockages and connects you to your heart. Keep breathing into the heart throughout the Invocation as you unite with Divine Mother and the Great Beings of the universe. Then begin the healing sequence.

Doing the Heart Exercise and then going right into the Invocation helps you connect to Divine Mother, who is actually conducting the healing. This process is designed to move you out of your small self and settle you into your heart.

Invocation of the Divine Beings

Start by saying:

I am Whole. I am One with God. I am One in the Infinite Wholeness of all that is. I call upon Almighty Mother-Father God and all of the beautiful expressions of Divine Love who know and live the Wholeness of Divine Truth.

I call upon these Great Divine Beings now …

Here, name those Great Beings who recognize their Wholeness and Oneness with God. Below is a list of some of the Divine Ones the author calls upon. It is not necessary to invite all of them. You may call upon the names below or only those who are familiar to you. Or just call upon Divine Mother or Mother-Father God.

I call upon the presence of Divine Mother in Her many aspects. I call upon Mother Mary (Christian), **Shekhina** (Jewish), **the Divine Presence of Fatima** (Islam), **Mother Lakshmi, Saraswati, Durga, Kali, Parvati** (Hindu). **I invite Tara and Quan Yin** (Buddhist), **Amaterasu** (Shinto), **White Buffalo Calf Woman** (Native American). **I call upon Gaia, Mother Earth, and Prakriti, Mother Nature. I invite all the expressions of Divine Mother from the world's traditions of Truth.**

I invite those Great Beings and Master Teachers around whom many of the world's spiritual traditions have grown. I call upon Jesus Christ and the Holy Spirit (Christian), **Abraham and Moses** [Jewish], **the Divine Presence of Mohammed** (Islam), **Lord Buddha** (Buddhist), **Lao Tzu** (Taoist), **Lord Krishna, Lord Ram, Lord Vishnu, Lord Shiva, Lord Brahma** (Hindu).

I call upon the Archangels: Archangels Michael, Gabriel, Raphael, Uriel, Zadkiel, Chamuel, Jophiel, Metatron, and all Archangels. (You may wish to add others.)

I invite the Ascended Masters: Babaji, Sananda, Serapis Bey, Saint Germain, Brother Francis of Assisi, Lady Nada, and all the Ascended Masters. (You may wish to add others.)

I invite the Gurus (Spiritual Teachers). (Name those fully enlightened Gurus who are significant in your life.)

Continue with:

There is a protective sphere of Holy Light surrounding me now, creating a sacred space. Archangel Michael and his legions of angels guard and protect this sacred space, so that only the energies of the Archangels, Ascended Masters, and Beings of Light holding the Wholeness of Divine Truth may enter this space. Archangel Michael stands in front of me, behind me, to the right of me, to the left of me, above me, and below me. I am safe and protected within this sacred sphere of Holy Light.

The loving, liquid, golden, healing substance of Divine Love is continually pouring into me throughout this healing session, allowing all the healing, lifting, and energy shifting to be smooth, comfortable, and complete.

I invite these Great Divine Beings to be present here now, to lift and heal me.

If there is a specific issue say:

Please heal the issue of _____

Name whatever you want to have healed. If there is not a specific issue at this time, continue with the healing sequence and know that the healing will be for your highest good in all areas.

Thank you Divine Mother, and so it is.

Softening Exercise

This exercise uses the power of attention and intention. The process is to move the attention to a specific place with the intention to soften there.

Softening is a relaxing or letting go of rigid boundaries. You are putting your attention on a specific place and then softening the boundaries of that place, letting your awareness flow beyond the boundaries.

Read the steps of the exercise, practicing it while you read it. Let your attention go to the area of the body named and soften there. The intent to soften is enough; don't try to make it happen.

Go slowly and pause each time you soften.

Here is the process:

> Soften in the heart …
> Soften in the heart center, not just the heart organ, but the whole chest area.
> Move your attention to the throat, soften in the throat …
> Soften the boundaries of the throat.
> Move your attention to the brow, which includes the brow area and the place between the eyebrows, often called the third eye. The attention is on the brow area.
> Soften in the brow/third eye …
> Soften at the top of the head, the crown …
> Soften at the base of the spine in the same way as you have been doing in the other energy centers.
> Soften in the pelvic area, the area below the navel, letting go in the pelvic area.
> Soften in the navel …
> Soften in the solar plexus, the diaphragm area above the navel.
> Soften again in the heart …

Repeat the above sequence at least three more times, ending by softening in the heart. Then continue with the following sequence:

> Soften in the cells.
> Soften in the brain, letting the brain melt like butter on a hot day.
> Soften in the whole body.
> Soften in the space around the body, the auric field.
> Soften in the navel.
> Soften in the heart.

Finish by inwardly saying:

> **I am Whole and One with All That Is.**
> **Thank you Divine Mother, and so it is.**

Divine Light

Soften in the heart.

Pause for a moment after every sentence, and read slowly. Repeat any of these paragraphs more than once if desired.

Divine Light is pouring into me now. Divine Light is filling my energy field on every level. Divine Light is increasing within me now. I am receiving more and more Divine Light, moment by moment. Divine Light is healing every limitation within my energy system and opening me to Wholeness now.

Pause and continue reading slowly.

Divine Light is releasing all discord within my system now and opening me to more Divine Light. Divine Light is flooding my energy system now. I accept Divine Light within me now. I know that Divine Light is increasing its presence within my system and illuminating my entire energy field. The most refined, sublime quality of Light in creation is opening in my energy system and lifting my energy field into resonance with Sacred Light vibration.

Divine Light is healing me now. This Sacred Light is lifting, opening, cleansing, and healing my entire system, and allowing the presence of Light to increase within me now. Divine Light is filling every organ, tissue, cell, atom, and particle of my body. Divine Light continues filling me and healing my entire energy field. I am inundated, saturated, permeated, and penetrated with Divine Light.

Pause and continue to read slowly.

Divine Light is emerging from Source and overflowing on every level of my energy field, nourishing my system with more Divine Light. I am receiving wave after wave of Light. I am filled with Light. More Divine Light is awakening in my entire system and releasing all that is not Whole.

The Wholeness of Divine Light fills me now. All energies of limitation and lack are dissolving as Divine Light vibrates throughout my energy field. I am held in Divine Light. I am bathed in Divine Light. I am healed in Divine Light. I am lifted, opened, cleansed, and freed in Divine Light.

Thank you Divine Mother, and so it is.

Closing Holes in Your Aura

I call upon Divine Mother and Archangel Michael to close all doors, openings, holes, portals, and pathways anywhere in my multi-leveled energy system to all limited (*those that limit your Wholeness*) **planes, domains, dimensions, spheres, realms, and locations anywhere in creation.**

I command in the name of Divine Mother that all doors, openings, holes, portals, and pathways anywhere in my multi-leveled energy system are now closed and sealed to the following levels:

Go through the list one at a time and after naming each limited level say, **"Close!"** and see doors slam throughout all levels of your energy field. Then see, know, or feel the doors are closed and sealed.

> **I close doors to the astral plane ... CLOSE!** (Includes disembodied earthbound spirits)
>
> **I close doors to the limited extra-terrestrial entities ... CLOSE!**
>
> **I close doors to the inter-dimensional entities ... CLOSE!** (Other subtle life forms)
>
> **I close doors to false gods ... CLOSE!** (Anything you make more powerful than your Infinite Self)
>
> **I close doors to lost souls ... CLOSE!** (Beings who have lost their evolutionary path)
>
> **I close doors to negative thought forms ... CLOSE!**
>
> **I close doors to all dense, low-frequency beings ... CLOSE!**
>
> **I close doors to the fear and negativity in the world consciousness ... CLOSE!**
>
> **I close doors to all unknown limited beings ... CLOSE!**

Repeat from the authority of your Divine Self:

> **These doors, openings, holes, portals, and pathways are now closed and sealed, in the name and through the power of Divine Mother, in the name and through the power of Archangel Michael.**

Again, image doors closing and sealing all around you. Focused attention on the holes closing is important.

Then say:

> **Any energetic configurations or attracting mechanisms around these now closed holes and openings are dismantled, broken, dissolved, and released.**

I am now opening into my authentic Self and moving through my individual life with Grace, Power, and Divine Integrity.

See or feel or know that a strong shield of protective Light is all around you, very vibrant and powerful.

End by saying:

I am aligned with Truth. I am Whole.
Thank you Divine Mother, and so it is.

First Go Command

This Tool clears the discord and blockages that have accumulated in the subtle fields of your energy system and are compromising the full expression of your True Self.

Breathe into the heart. Say:

> **I call upon Divine Mother and all the Divine Beings to release and clear all discordant energies, blockages, and confusion from the following levels of my system.**

First, clear the <u>emotional level</u>.

Say lovingly but firmly from your Divine Authority, not from your small self:

> **I now address all blockages and discord at the emotional level of my energy field. Go into the Light. Go ... Go ... Go ... Go into the Light ...**

As needed, repeat:

> **Go into the Light. Go ... Go ... Go ... Go into the Light ... Go ... Go ... Go ... Go into the Light. In the name of God, I command you to go into the Light now.**

Continue repeating **"Go"** until you notice a shift, like a sense of expansion, a deep breath, or a settling indicating there has been a release.

You are clearing layers of your emotional system. By repeating **"Go into the Light"** over and over, you clear deeper and deeper layers. Keep repeating **"Go"** until you feel clear and complete at each level.

As you proceed, alternate saying **"Go"** with filling the level with Diving Light. Say:

> **Divine Light is filling the emotional level, Divine Light is pouring into the emotional level, Divine Light is saturating the emotional level, more and more Divine Light fills the emotional level.**

Then return to saying **"Go, Go into the Light ..."** until you sense that level is clear and complete.

Next, clear the <u>mental level</u>. Say:

> **I now address all blockages and discord at the mental level of my energy field. Go into the Light. Go, Go, Go ...**

At every level, follow the same instructions for clearing as stated above.

Now clear the <u>etheric level</u>. Say:

> **I now address all blockages and discord at the etheric level of my energy field. Go into the Light. Go, Go, Go ...**

Follow instructions as stated above.

Clear the <u>physical level</u>. Say:

> **I now address all blockages and discord at the physical level of my energy field. Go into the Light. Go, Go, Go ...**

Follow instructions as stated above.

Clear the <u>astral level</u>. Say:

> **I now address all blockages and discord at the astral level of my energy field Go into the Light. Go, Go, Go ...**

Follow instructions as stated above.

Clear the <u>causal level</u>. Say:

> **I now address all blockages and discord at the causal level of my energy field. Go into the Light. Go, Go, Go ...**

Follow instructions as stated above.

Clear the <u>celestial level</u>. Say:

> **I now address all blockages and discord at the celestial level of my energy field. Go into the Light. Go, Go, Go ...**

Follow instructions as stated above.

Clear the level of <u>Pure Spirit</u>. Pure Spirit is always clear. Here, we clear any mental, emotional, and spiritual misconceptions which limit the experience of this level. Say:

> **I now address all blockages and discord at the level of Pure Spirit. Go into the Light. Go, Go, Go ...**

Follow instructions as stated above.

Finally, clear the <u>Avenue of Awareness</u>, which governs the way life is perceived. Say:

> **I now address all blockages and discord in the Avenue of Awareness. Go into the Light. Go, Go, Go …**

Follow instructions as stated above.

Then conclude by saying:

> **All limited energies, entities, and negative programs are now released and let go on every level of my energy system. All doors, openings, holes, portals, or pathways to these areas are now closed and sealed.**

See, know, and feel your aura is strong and powerful.

Then say:

> **I am now opening into the Wholeness of my Authentic Self, and it is flowing through my individual life with Grace, Power, and Divine Integrity.**
>
> **Thank you Divine Mother, and so it is.**

Break Command

Breathe into the heart and center in your Divine Self, which is in the heart. Continue breathing into the heart and say the following words:

I call upon Divine Mother, Archangel Michael, and all the Divine Beings to break, shatter, and dissolve all old patterns, grids, frameworks, structures, and multidimensional matrices that are limiting me or holding negative energies in my system. These structures are now broken, shattered, cracked up, dissolved, released, and completely let go throughout my multidimensional energy system.

Then take some deep breaths through the heart and chest to activate the life force for healing and transforming your system.

Say the word **"Break!"** out loud (silently if other people not involved in the healing are nearby) and image these structures breaking, shattering, and dissolving. Your imaging tells the energy what to do.

Repeat the word **"Break!"** lovingly but firmly from your Divine Authority, not from your small self.

Say **"Break! Break! Break …"** many times as deeper layers of your system are cleared of the old structures, while continuously imaging the structures breaking and collapsing.

As you say **"Break,"** your voice may soften as you reach the deeper levels of your system. At some point, it will be appropriate to say **"Break"** inwardly. Keep repeating **"Break,"** imaging and feeling the structures dismantling at deeper, more subtle levels. Soften and let go as you break these structures.

In addition to saying **"Break, Break,"** you can use the words, **"Shatter," "Burst," "Smash," "Dissolve," "Melt," "Collapse,"** or other words commanding the dissolution of the old stuck vibrational patterns and structures.

Remember to keep softening and letting go, knowing that the Divine power is doing the breaking, not your individual will.

Notice your energy as you do this and continue until you have a sense of new freedom and expansion in your energy field.

End with:

These old grids, frameworks, and structures are now completely broken, shattered, and dissolved and I am Whole. I am aligned with Truth.

Thank you Divine Mother, and so it is.

Finish by bringing in the Divine Nectar, the liquid Love, to nourish your system and fill the space, now that these grids of untruth are gone. It is the next Tool in the sequence.

Divine Nectar

Breathe into the heart. Soften and let go of any tension. Allow the heart to expand.

Say:

> I am One in the Wholeness of all that is. I am receiving the Love of Divine Mother soaking into me as a nectar-like substance, the pure essence of Divine Love.
>
> I am filling with Divine Nectar now. This Divine Nectar, the essence of Divine Love, is healing me. I am receiving this Liquid Love on every level of my entire energy field. Divine Nectar is pouring into me. I am bathed in Divine Nectar. I am filled with Divine Nectar. I am healed by Divine Nectar.
>
> Liquid Love is healing me as it flows through my system. I am soaking in the sacred Nectar. My heart is being soothed by Liquid Love. The loving flow of Divine Nectar is filling my body, healing every cell, every organ, and every system. My head is filling with Divine Nectar, calming my thoughts, soothing my brain, soaking into my cells. I am filled with Liquid Love.

(Pause and notice the Divine Nectar. Stay soft and centered in the Divine Self in your heart while saying these words.)

> I am letting go of harmful thoughts. I am healing my thinking process. I am opening to Divine Nectar in my head and in my heart. The Nectar is continuing to flood my body. I am healing in this essence of Divine Mother's Love. Divine Nectar is filling me with Liquid Love, and my system is healing the sadness, pain, and suffering.
>
> I am allowing Divine Nectar to increase within me now. I am filling with this Nectar of Love. I am releasing all fear and trusting Divine Nectar to heal everything that is afraid. The waves of Liquid Love are flowing into me, saturating me with their loving caress. I am receiving Divine Nectar.
>
> I open to the flowing Nectar and allow its waves of Love to fill my heart, my body, my mind, and my energy field. I accept Divine Nectar within me now.

Repeat this as often as desired to enrich your system with the healing, soothing presence of Divine Nectar.

> **Thank you Divine Mother, and so it is.**

Divine Love

Soften in the heart.

Pause for a moment after every sentence, and read slowly. Repeat any of these paragraphs more than once if desired.

> **Divine Love is pouring into me now. I am receiving Divine Love on every level of my existence. I am opening to allow Divine Love to fill me and overflow in my life now.**
>
> **I accept Divine Love within me now. I am inundated, saturated, permeated, and penetrated with Divine Love. Divine Love fills me again and again on deeper and deeper levels of my existence.**

Have a gentle awareness of Divine Love.

Read slowly and pause between each sentence.

> **I am healing in Divine Love. The Love of Divine Mother is pouring into every atom, cell, organ, and system of my entire physical body. I am flooded with Divine Love, bathed in Divine Love, cleansed by Divine Love.**
>
> **I open and accept Divine Love within me now on every level of my life expression.**
>
> **The lively, dynamic energy of Divine Love is cleansing, dissolving, and transmuting all energies of lack and limitation within my energy system. I am opening to the presence of more and more life energy of Divine Love. The vital life energy of Divine Love is transmuting all energies of discord within me now. Radiant, vibrant Divine Love is erasing all error conditioning, all error patterning, all limited belief systems, and all limiting self-concepts.**
>
> **Divine Love is opening in the deepest areas of my energy field. The oldest, most lost, forgotten, ignored areas of my system are receiving Divine Love. Divine Love is welling up from deep within, dissolving all blocked energy within my energy field. More and more Divine Love is opening within me now. Old ancestral patterning is releasing now. All old frequencies, from this life or any other, this dimension or any other, are releasing now. Old frequencies, old conditioning, old energies from the past are letting go, releasing, and lifting.**

Notice and allow. Keep letting go to allow the Divine Love.

Read slowly and pause between each sentence.

Divine Love is radiant within me now. Divine Love is increasing its presence within my energy field. The life energy of Divine Love is pulsating within my energy system now, in unison with the heartbeat of the Creator. I am radiant with Divine Love.

I am One with the fullness of Divine Mother's Love.

I am moving in the Wholeness of Divine Love as Divine Love creates more and more Love within me now.

Thank you Divine Mother, and so it is.

Cutting Binding Ties

Breathe into the heart.

I ask Divine Mother and Archangel Michael with his Blue Flame Sword of Truth to lovingly cut all binding ties, hooks, threads, cords, attachments, and any other kind of tie that may be limiting me in any way.

These ties are now cut between myself and _____ [name]. (Name specific persons, places, events, situations, or conditions where you have felt limited, bound, or attached in any way. If you are completing a full healing sequence, cut ties between yourself and everything that has been released during the healing session.)

Then say:

These binding ties, hooks, threads, cords, and attachments are now lovingly cut by Archangel Michael and his Blue Flame Sword of Truth. They are completely and thoroughly cut, lifted, healed, removed, dissolved, and released from every level of my multi-leveled energy field.

Next say:

I ask Divine Mother and Archangel Michael to release all these ties and attachments from me now, layer, by layer, by layer.

I allow these binding ties and attachments to be let go and transmuted into Light by Divine Mother now, layer, by layer, by layer.

These ties are lovingly cut layer, by layer, by layer, by layer, by layer, by layer, by layer throughout my entire vibrational field.

Image the ties being cut.

Even the subtlest ties are cut, lifted, healed, released, and dissolved layer, by layer, by layer, by layer.

Repeat:

They are cut layer, by layer, by layer, by layer …

… until you sense the release is complete. The repetition is important because you are cutting ties through every level of your multi-leveled energy system.

Then say:

I am free.

Finish with:

I know that I am Whole and One with All That Is.
Thank you Divine Mother, and so it is.

Closing a Divine Mother Healing Session

Breathe into your heart and say:

Thank you, Divine Mother and all the Beings of Wholeness, for the purification and alignment with Truth that I have received from you today.

My heart is open and receiving your Divine Presence. I am moving with you through this day.

The Love that you have for me is now resonating throughout my body, mind, and heart as I conduct my life in alignment with Divine Truth.

I now allow Divine Love to flow into my physical body as I become active and engaged with the environment.

Begin to gently move and stretch, slowly bringing the body from a resting state into activity.

I come into activity balanced and integrated with my physical surroundings.

I know that Divine Mother is with me and that all is well.

Say the following affirmations, speaking with confidence, knowing that it is so:

I am alert. I am clear. I am balanced within myself and with my outer environment.

I am Whole. I am One with All That Is. I am divinely protected by Divine Mother's Love.

I close all doors, openings, and holes in my energy field to the limited planes of existence now.

I close to the astral plane (pause a moment and say, "Close"); **to the limited extra-terrestrial regions, "Close"; to the inter-dimensional realms, "Close"; to the lost souls, "Close"; to the false gods, "Close"; to the negative thought forms, "Close"; to the heavy, dense energy beings, "Close"; and to the race-mind consciousness of Mother Earth, "Close." All doors, openings, holes to these regions are now closed and sealed in the name and through the power of Divine Mother.**

Image doors closing around you.

Then say:

My aura and body of light are radiant with Divine Presence.

Pause for a moment here to fill the aura with the Light. Sense, feel, know, image, and intend that your auric field, for about ten feet all around you, is brilliant with Light, sparkling with Light, glowing with Light, empowered and vibrant with Divine Light.

Then say:

I am aligned with Truth.
I am Whole.

End with three grounding breaths:

Take a deep breath into your body, bringing all of the Divine Love, Light, Truth, and Grace to fill your physical body, and then as you exhale, connect with Mother Earth by sending the energy into Mother Earth beneath your feet. Again, take another deep breath, bringing the Divine Energy into your body and exhale into Mother Earth. Then take one more breath, filling the physical body with Divine Energy, and as you exhale, ground yourself on Mother Earth.

Now say:

I am now moving through my life with Grace, Power, and Divine Integrity.
Thank you Divine Mother, and so it is.

Take any additional time you need to stretch, open your eyes slowly, and integrate with the environment.

Chapter 13

Mini-Session

A Mini-Session is a quick and focused way to bring yourself out of any surface confusion and agitation. It can be used as a pick-me-up during the day. It closes and strengthens your aura and heals the surface level disruptions. It is designed to clear negative, discordant energies, connect you to your center, and open you to the experience of mental clarity with a joyful heart. A deeper healing is recommended when time allows.

Heart Exercise – Mini-Form

To start a Divine Mother Mini-Session:

> Breathe into your heart a few times. Center in your heart before beginning the Mini-Session.

Invoke Divine Mother

Invoke Divine Mother by saying Her name.

Say:

> **I call upon Divine Mother. Be with me, Divine Mother.**

Breathe into your heart a few more times.

Say:

> **Divine Mother, connect to me. We are One.**

Know that Divine Mother is with you. Just by saying Her name, you activate Her Presence around you. Intend to connect with Her.

Then continue with the Closing Holes in Your Aura Tool.

Closing Holes in Your Aura

I call upon Divine Mother and Archangel Michael to close all doors, openings, holes, portals, and pathways anywhere in my multi-leveled energy system to all limited (*those that limit your Wholeness*) **planes, domains, dimensions, spheres, realms, and locations anywhere in creation.**

I command in the name of Divine Mother that all doors, openings, holes, portals, and pathways anywhere in my multi-leveled energy system are now closed and sealed to the following levels:

Go through the list one at a time and after naming each limited level say, **"Close!"** and see doors slam throughout all levels of your energy field. Then see, know, or feel the doors are closed and sealed.

> **I close doors to the astral plane ... CLOSE!** (Includes disembodied earthbound spirits)
>
> **I close doors to the limited extra-terrestrial entities ... CLOSE!**
>
> **I close doors to the inter-dimensional entities ... CLOSE!** (Other subtle life forms)
>
> **I close doors to false gods ... CLOSE!** (Anything you make more powerful than your Infinite Self)
>
> **I close doors to lost souls ... CLOSE!** (Beings who have lost their evolutionary path)
>
> **I close doors to negative thought forms ... CLOSE!**
>
> **I close doors to all dense, low-frequency beings ... CLOSE!**
>
> **I close doors to the fear and negativity in the world consciousness ... CLOSE!**
>
> **I close doors to all unknown limited beings ... CLOSE!**

Repeat from the authority of your Divine Self:

> **These doors, openings, holes, portals, and pathways are now closed and sealed, in the name and through the power of Divine Mother, in the name and through the power of Archangel Michael.**

Again, image doors closing and sealing all around you. Focused attention on the holes closing is important.

Then say:

> **Any energetic configurations or attracting mechanisms around these now closed holes and openings are dismantled, broken, dissolved, and released.**

I am now opening into my authentic Self and moving through my individual life with Grace, Power, and Divine Integrity.

See or feel or know that a strong shield of protective Light is all around you, very vibrant and powerful.

End by saying:

I am aligned with Truth. I am Whole.
Thank you Divine Mother, and so it is.

First Go Command

This Tool clears the discord and blockages that have accumulated in the subtle fields of your energy system and are compromising the full expression of your True Self.

Breathe into the heart. Say:

> **I call upon Divine Mother and all the Divine Beings to release and clear all discordant energies, blockages, and confusion from the following levels of my system.**

First, clear the <u>emotional level</u>.

Say lovingly but firmly from your Divine Authority, not from your small self:

> **I now address all blockages and discord at the emotional level of my energy field. Go into the Light. Go … Go … Go … Go into the Light …**

As needed, repeat:

> **Go into the Light. Go … Go … Go … Go into the Light … Go … Go … Go … Go into the Light. In the name of God, I command you to go into the Light now.**

Continue repeating **"Go"** until you notice a shift, like a sense of expansion, a deep breath, or a settling indicating there has been a release.

You are clearing layers of your emotional system. By repeating **"Go into the Light"** over and over, you clear deeper and deeper layers. Keep repeating **"Go"** until you feel clear and complete at each level.

As you proceed, alternate saying **"Go"** with filling the level with Diving Light. Say:

> **Divine Light is filling the emotional level, Divine Light is pouring into the emotional level, Divine Light is saturating the emotional level, more and more Divine Light fills the emotional level.**

Then return to saying **"Go, Go into the Light …"** until you sense that level is clear and complete.

Next, clear the <u>mental level</u>. Say:

> **I now address all blockages and discord at the mental level of my energy field. Go into the Light. Go, Go, Go …**

At every level, follow the same instructions for clearing as stated above.

Now clear the <u>etheric level</u>. Say:

> **I now address all blockages and discord at the etheric level of my energy field. Go into the Light. Go, Go, Go ...**

Follow instructions as stated above.

Clear the <u>physical level</u>. Say:

> **I now address all blockages and discord at the physical level of my energy field. Go into the Light. Go, Go, Go ...**

Follow instructions as stated above.

Clear the <u>astral level</u>. Say:

> **I now address all blockages and discord at the astral level of my energy field Go into the Light. Go, Go, Go ...**

Follow instructions as stated above.

Clear the <u>causal level</u>. Say:

> **I now address all blockages and discord at the causal level of my energy field. Go into the Light. Go, Go, Go ...**

Follow instructions as stated above.

Clear the <u>celestial level</u>. Say:

> **I now address all blockages and discord at the celestial level of my energy field. Go into the Light. Go, Go, Go ...**

Follow instructions as stated above.

Clear the level of <u>Pure Spirit</u>. Pure Spirit is always clear. Here, we clear any mental, emotional, and spiritual misconceptions which limit the experience of this level. Say:

> **I now address all blockages and discord at the level of Pure Spirit. Go into the Light. Go, Go, Go ...**

Follow instructions as stated above.

Finally, clear the <u>Avenue of Awareness</u>, which governs the way life is perceived. Say:

> **I now address all blockages and discord in the Avenue of Awareness. Go into the Light. Go, Go, Go …**

Follow instructions as stated above.

Then conclude by saying:

> **All limited energies, entities, and negative programs are now released and let go on every level of my energy system. All doors, openings, holes, portals, or pathways to these areas are now closed and sealed.**

See, know, and feel your aura is strong and powerful.

Then say:

> **I am now opening into the Wholeness of my Authentic Self, and it is flowing through my individual life with Grace, Power, and Divine Integrity.**
>
> **Thank you Divine Mother, and so it is.**

Ascending Light

Breathe into the heart.

Ascending Light is lifting me now. Ascending Light is pouring into my energy system. Ascending Light is moving throughout my multi-leveled energy field. Ascending Light is resonating on every level of my system, opening me to more Ascending Light. I accept Ascending Light within me now, in every aspect of my life expression.

I am radiant with Ascending Light and Ascending Light is increasing its presence within me moment by moment. I am being transformed in Ascending Light so that I may become all that I am capable of becoming.

Ascending Light is lifting and clearing all ancestral patterning within my energy system. Ascending Light is freeing my system from all limiting energies and frequencies. I allow Ascending Light to free me now.

Ascending Light is filling my cells. It is healing my cells as they vibrate with Ascending Light. More and more Ascending Light is saturating my cells now.

Breathe into the heart. Have the intention to soften and allow the Ascending Light.

Ascending Light is entering my DNA. Ascending Light is freeing my DNA and restructuring it in Divine Truth. My DNA is overflowing with Ascending Light. I am being lifted, opened, cleansed, and healed in Ascending Light. I am filling with Ascending Light. I am accepting Ascending Light, and it is transforming me now. I allow Ascending Light to fill me now.

I am lifted, opened, cleansed, and freed in Ascending Light now.

I am Whole. I am One with All That Is. I am filled with Ascending Light.

You can repeat this as often as you like to raise your vibration with Ascending Light.

Chapter 14

Specialized Tools

Self-Love Exercise

Call yourself by name, and say inwardly:

> **I love you, _____ [your name]. You are beautiful. I love you with all my heart. You are perfect in my eyes. You are wonderful. I love everything about you. You are good. You are wise. You are dear to me.**
>
> **You are _____.**

Continue with more compliments. Engage your heart; speak to yourself from your heart. Say what you want to hear; for example:

> **You are kind. You are loving. You are capable. You are smart. You are strong. You are generous. You are fun to be with. You are thoughtful. You are honest. You care about people. You are creative. You are graceful. You are worthy. You are joyful. You are brilliant. You are radiant with Light. You are courageous.**

Don't qualify what you are saying by adding, "You are loveable when you are nice to people" or "You are good some of the time." Love all parts of yourself without qualification or justification.

Each person may wish to hear something different; tailor your words to what is meaningful to you.

Often negative or self-critical thoughts come up during the practice. If this happens, go into your heart and stand up for yourself. Don't allow yourself to be bullied by critical thoughts. Say from the conviction of your heart, "That's not true—I am good, I am honest, I am kind, I am loving," or other appropriate words. Your heart is where your courage is. Speak from the heart and the critical mind will back off. Don't accept any criticism or argument from the intellect/ego/mind. If it persists, say, "In the name of God, I command you to go into the Light."

Continue speaking to yourself lovingly, complimenting yourself by saying the things that you wish your partner, family member, employer, or best friend would say to you. You know what you want them to say. Say it to yourself. It will deeply nourish you.

Continue speaking these loving words until you become relaxed and receptive to them in your heart. Let them soak in and nurture your whole being.

Notice the good feeling that is generated. Sink into it, melt into it, and let it embrace you. Become the good feeling you have created.

As you melt and let go, you become softened and expanded. Continue the process until you feel relaxed, safe, and loved.

Tips for Getting Started

If you're having difficulty with this exercise:

1. Pretend Divine Mother is saying the words to you. She loves you unconditionally.
2. Pretend somebody who cares deeply for you is saying these words.
3. What you are saying does not have to make logical sense. You don't have to give reasons to prove what you are saying. (For example: "I'm good because I gave money to the homeless." Just say, "I am good.")
4. Don't get stuck in details. You want this to flow. Talk from your heart, not your mind. The heart has no need for details or proof.
5. If the negative self-talk is so strong that it's hard to get past it, then use other Divine Mother Tools like the Go Command or the Break Command. You may even need a personal healing session from a trained Divine Mother Healing practitioner.
6. Record yourself speaking the words of self-love. Play it any time. It is especially effective when heard before going to sleep at night and when awakening in the morning.
7. Begin by using the Creating the Flow of Love Exercise to get the love flowing between you and Divine Mother. Then shift into saying to yourself, "I love you _____ [your name]" and continue with the Self-Love Exercise.

Creating the Flow of Love

This is an exchange of love between you and Divine Mother.

Instructions from Divine Mother:

I want you to activate the flow of Love between us. Be Me. At the deepest level of your life, we are One, so it is okay to "pretend" to be Me. I want you to use your inner voice and speak My words of love to yourself, either out loud or silently.

Pretending to be Me, say in your voice:

I love you, _____ [your name].

Then, as yourself, say back to Me:

I love you, Divine Mother.

I say in your voice:

I love you, _____ [your name].

Notice the effect of that statement inside of you. It is very subtle, but you <u>can</u> notice My love.

Now, I want you to say that back to Me:

I love you, Divine Mother.

And notice the love flowing to Me, like a wave on the ocean. We will exchange "I love you's."

You say in your voice, being Me:

I love you, _____ [your name].

Then say, being you:

I love you, Divine Mother.

Notice the energy ebbing and flowing between us.

Continue saying **"I love you, _____** [your name], **I love you, Divine Mother, I love you, _____** [your name], **I love you, Divine Mother ...,"** speaking back and forth this way until you feel drenched in My love and connected to Me. This is a way to activate our personal relationship.

The purpose of this exercise is to get the flow of love moving between us strongly enough so that you can feel it.

If you feel any resistance or mental objections when you do this exercise, use the Go Command or Break Command to dissolve the resistance. Keep coming back to the "I love you's."

Heart Exercise – Long Form

Read this with the intention to do it as you read.

Breathe into the heart center, not just the heart organ, but the whole chest area. Breathe as if the breath is coming through the front of the chest into the heart and soften in the heart to receive the breath. Allow the heart to open, like a flower opening its petals, to receive the warm, soft breath.

If it is difficult to keep your attention in the heart, take many strong, slow, deep breaths (10 to 15) into the chest area. The deep breaths quiet mental activity and then it's easier to focus attention on the heart.

The breath carries life energy. Soften in the heart as it receives the breath, and notice the flow of breath moving into the heart center.

Put attention on the heart center, which is the whole chest area, not just the heart organ. Notice if there is any tightness or discomfort there. If there is, breathe into it, allowing the breath to flow through it, opening it up, and moving the stream of breath through the discomfort. Continue this process until the discomfort dissolves.

If there is no discomfort, breathe into whatever you notice there, whether it's physical, emotional, visual, or vibrational.

When the discomfort dissolves, or when the experience changes, notice what presents next in the heart. Whatever you notice, breathe into it.

If you do not notice anything, breathe into the "nothing" and notice the movement of breath flowing into the "nothing."

Layers of the heart will unfold as you continue the exercise, revealing deeper blocks or deeper clarity depending on whether your heart is blocked or open. Keep noticing what presents. Even if it is a comfortable or pleasant sensation, breathe into that. Everything that presents is asking you to breathe into it. You are healing and awakening your heart by opening it to the flow of life energy carried on the breath. This flow not only releases and dissolves blocks to the movement of life energy through your heart, it also connects you to your True Self. These blocks have kept your heart constricted, tense, and disconnected from your True Self.

The process is as follows:

1. Breathe into the heart center.
2. What do you notice?

3. Breathe into whatever you notice until it changes.

4. When it changes, notice what presents next, and breathe into that.

5. Continue breathing into whatever the heart presents. There will be layers of the heart unfolding as you breathe into it.

6. This can continue for as long as desired, but it's best if you proceed until there is a sense of peace.

This is the Heart Exercise. Practice it often, for as long as you can, eyes closed in quiet times or eyes open in activity. Some people use the heart exercise as a meditation; others use it as a relaxation technique. Doing it for a few minutes or even seconds can center you and provide comfort and peace.

Spinning Ascending Light

You can transform the energy of any uncomfortable experience by spinning Ascending Light in it. The spiraling Light lifts your vibrational frequency out of density. Density is often experienced as depression, fear, unworthiness, hopelessness, helplessness, or despair. You can be lifted with the Ascending Light spiral out of these experiences. It takes focus and attention. Here is the process:

Breathe into your heart and soften there.

Allow a spiral of Ascending Light to spin in any area of density. Spin it in the places where you are feeling heavy, dense, dull, or stuck. Expressions of these conditions often appear as pain, frustration, self-criticism, negative thoughts, or hostility. If you want to lift the vibration of your whole physical body, spin Light in the whole body.

You can imagine, picture, see, sense, or feel the spiral spinning like a whirlwind or tornado of Light.

Don't be concerned about the direction of the spin, clockwise or counter-clockwise. The spin will spontaneously take the direction that is most needed for your support. The Divine Mind knows how to facilitate your intention to spin Ascending Light.

See, feel, or just know that the spiral is present and spinning upward.

Once you get the spiral going, allow it to spin faster and faster.

Then spin the Light even faster...like a golden tornado, constantly accelerating its velocity.

The spiral of Ascending Light is lifting you and freeing you from all dense, heavy vibrational frequencies.

Spin faster …

Accelerate the speed …

Accelerate faster …

Continue to accelerate the spin faster again and again …

Soften and relax while you spin, keeping the attention on the spin while staying open and alert. Be easy with no strain. Keep softening anywhere in your system that starts to tense or strain. If you ever start to get a headache, soften and breathe into the heart.

Spin the Light for as long as it takes until the density is lifted and the stuck energy is freed. You will eventually notice a shift. Until then, keep accelerating the spin. It can take some time, but when the stuck energy breaks there is an expansion, a sense of freedom, and a letting go.

Finish with:

Thank you Divine Mother, and so it is.

Aura Empowerment

Breathe into the heart.

As you say this Aura Empowerment technique, see, feel, know, image, or intend that the Light is doing what you are saying during every statement.

> **My aura, the space around my body for at least 10 feet in all directions, is filled with Light. Divine Light beams from my core and fills my auric field, like the rays of a brilliant sun.**

> **I am radiant with Light. My aura is sparkling with Light, brilliant with Light, glowing with Light, blazing with Light.**

Continue to image this while saying it. Notice it, feel it, see it, know it.

> **My auric field is vibrant with Divine Light and alive with life force. Divine Light is radiating from my core. It protects me and creates a shield of Light within me and around me wherever I go and in whatever I do.**

> **It remains powerful and strong as I interact with others. Nothing limited can penetrate the power of my auric field. It is holding me in a place of safety.**

Notice the Light and feel the safety.

> **I am Whole. The power in me comes from my Infinite Source.**
> **I am One with All That Is.**
> **Thank you Divine Mother, and so it is.**

Note: As an added protection at any time, you can revisit the Closing Holes in Your Aura Tool on page 55 to firmly close your aura to all limited subtle energies.

Canceling Spells and Curses

Breathe into your heart and center there.

Step 1:

Fortify yourself by calling on your Divine Friends from the Invocation of Divine Beings. Create the Protective Sphere of Light from the Invocation around you, with Archangel Michael standing on all sides of you. Then use the Closing Holes in Your Aura technique. Now you are strong, centered, and held by Divine Mother.

Step 2:

Say out loud in a firm voice and with conviction:

> **I ask Divine Mother, Archangel Michael, Jesus Christ, and the Company of Heaven, to cancel and release all spells, enchantments, curses, oaths, hexes, sorcery, pacts, bindings, and the like, and all dark magic that I may have ever been a part of, either given or received, in my multidimensional existence, in all former lifetimes either on this planet or in any other domain or dimension.**

Step 3:

Then declare with the power of Divine authority:

> **These are all now dissolved, released, canceled, broken, made null and void in the name and through the power of Jesus Christ, in the name and through the power of Archangel Michael, in the name and through the power of Divine Mother.**

Say firmly, pausing after each command:

> **They are all now broken … shattered … smashed … dismantled … dissolved, made null and void …**

> **And all subtle negative entities holding them in place must go into the Light! … Go, Break, Go, Break, Shatter, Smash …**

Repeat the commands **"Break! Shatter! Dissolve!"** and **"Go into the Light!"** again and again. You are healing layer after layer of the spell or curse. Keep going until you feel openness and expansion in your energy.

Go back and repeat this Divine Mother Tool from the beginning, three or four times as needed, consistently calling on the support of your Divine Friends, and reading all the way through to the "Break" and "Go" section.

The effectiveness of this Tool is in its repetitions, as deeper and deeper layers of the spell or curse are being broken.

Step 4:

After a period of saying **"Break"** and **"Go,"** test whether the negative energy has cleared. See the list of different types of spells and curses below. One by one, go over each to see if any of them still has a "charge" or an "agitated vibration" attached to it. If yes, continue to use **"Go!"** and **"Break!"** numerous times for that particular one. When the curse, spell, or oath is neutralized, there will no longer be a "charge" around it, only peace.

Check for a "charge" from each word below by saying:

> **I ask Divine Mother to heal all** _____ [name spell type].

Then pause and hold the word in your awareness determining if it is clear. Go through the list and heal where still needed until all words are completely neutral with no vibrational agitation around them.

List:

> **Spells** … heal if necessary with the Go and Break Commands.
> **Enchantments** … heal if necessary.
> **Curses** … heal if necessary.
> **Oaths** … heal if necessary.
> **Hexes** … heal if necessary.
> **Sorcery** … heal if necessary.
> **Pacts** … heal if necessary.
> **Bindings and the like** … heal if necessary.
> **All dark magic** … heal if necessary.

Important:

Repeat **"Break"** and **"Go"** emphatically after each one until you are certain that the energy has been dissolved and the vibration broken for each negative issue. Keep letting go into the Infinite Source, softening as you do this.

When you are satisfied that all the words in this list are free of negative charge, continue to heal your energy field by reading the following Healing Tools in the order listed:

Divine Nectar
Ascending Light
Closing Holes in Your Aura
Binding Tie Cut - Cut the ties to everything that has been healed.
Divine Grace
Aura Empowerment

Then end with:

Thank you Divine Mother, and so it is.

Note: If you don't feel completely cleared, go through the entire Divine Mother Healing Tool sequence from beginning to end. It will lift your vibration out of the realm of these issues.

If you desire assistance, Divine Mother certified practitioners are available at www.DivineMotherOnline.net.

Light Exercise

This exercise intensifies Light in any area that you wish to transform. It could be in a relationship, legal situation, diseased part of your body, or anything else that needs to be healed and lifted for the highest good.

Start by Setting Your Intention

Make a statement about what you wish to transform. For example: "I am bringing Light into my relationship to transform it for the highest good for all concerned." Divine Intelligence will know how to create highest good. You don't have to worry about it or have an agenda about it with your individual will. Let Divine Will operate here.

Preparation

This exercise is an intention in the Wholeness of awareness. It's important to be settled and peaceful when you begin.

If you decide to use this exercise as part of a vibrational healing session, you will already be settled.

If using it outside a healing sequence, begin with the Softening Exercise to become centered and quiet. When you are settled, then begin.

First Stage:

> **Allow Light …**
> **Allow more Light …**
> **Allow more Light …**
> **More Light …**
> **More Light …**
> **More Light …**
> **Fill with Light …**
> **Overflow with Light …** (Keep allowing more Light until you feel it is time to shift.)

Second Stage:

> **Hold Light …**
> **Hold …**
> **Hold …**
> **Hold …**
> **Hold Light …**
> Soften, no strain, continue to Hold Light.

Hold ... Hold ... Hold Light ...
Hold ... (until you feel it is time to shift)

Third Stage:

> **Let go ...**
> **Let go ...**
> **Let go ...**
> **Let go and fall into the Infinite Source ...**
> **Keep letting go ...**

Begin again with the First Stage.

Repeat the three stages three times or more to completely saturate the situation with Light.

Conclusion:

> **Then let go ...**
> **Allow ...**
> **Be ...**
> **Trust ...**

Finish with:

> **Thank you Divine Mother, and so it is.**

Divine Joy

Breathe into the heart and soften.

The power of Divine Joy is transforming my life now. I am filled with Divine Joy. I am embraced by Divine Joy.

The Joy of Divine Mother's Love is filling me now. I am receiving the Joy of Divine Mother's Presence within me now. I know that I am loved and cherished unconditionally. I experience the Joy of being held and cradled in Divine Mother's arms.

Divine Joy is my constant state. I am soaked and saturated with Divine Joy. Joy is always available to me as I live my everyday life. I am overjoyed by the beauty of the earth around me. My life is saturated with Joy in every moment. Divine Joy is an indelible part of me now. I am living a life of wonder and Joy.

Thank you Divine Mother, and so it is.

Chapter 15

Healing on the Run

You can use Divine Mother's Healing Tools in quick abbreviated versions throughout a busy day. They will help dissolve negative energy and break through blocks you may encounter. You are becoming a Master of Energy, so you can apply these Tools and techniques to all situations in your life to make life smoother, easier, and more joyful.

The shortened Tools are quick fixes, and do not replace the deeper healing and long-term transformational effect gained by using the entire healing system. However, the quick healing methods below can smooth a rough incident and instantly bless those around you.

1. Call on a Divine Being.

Say or think the name of any Divine Being, calling upon God in a personal form. (Divine Mother, Mother Mary, Jesus Christ, Archangel Michael, or any other Great Being who recognizes they are Whole and One with God). This immediately connects you to this Divine Being for help and protection. This connection and assistance will be enough to shift the direction of the situation.

From Invocation of the Divine Beings

2. Breathe into the Heart.

Breathe into the heart and notice the whole chest area. Continue to breathe into whatever is tight or tense in the chest area until it dissolves and you experience peace.

From the Heart Exercise

3. Pour Divine Light into a Person or a Situation.

Say or think, "Divine Light is pouring into _____ [a person or situation]," and other phrases from the Divine Light Tool. Then imagine or visualize this happening. You can do this for people, events, conditions, or whenever there is tension, anger, fear, or other agitation. This fills the situation with Light.

From Divine Light

4. Bombs of Light

In any situation that is heavy, stuck, or negative, a quick way to bring Light into it is to burst or explode Light. This works effectively to "lighten" a situation. Imagine Light bursting or exploding in the negativity of a person, group, or world conflict. Exploding Light increases and expands Light.

From Divine Light

5. Say "Go!" to Discord and Negativity.

Say, "Go" whenever sensing the energy of negativity around you or another person. State the command, "Go! Go into the Light!" from the power of your God Self. You can say "Go" quietly inside if someone else is around.

From the Go Command

6. Break Grids of Untruth.

Inwardly, say "Break" several times and image the grids breaking whenever you notice yourself or someone else repeating a pattern of fear, anger, guilt, shame, or self-criticism. This is especially useful in family or business situations where old patterns repeat.

From the Break Command

7. Close Holes in Your Aura.

If you have been feeling fine and suddenly notice anger, heaviness, fatigue, or negativity, you may be experiencing the impact of other people's negative energies. Focus attention on closing holes in your auric field. Imagine or "see" holes closing around you. This will help you become self-contained and protected from discord in the environment.

From Closing Holes in Your Aura

8. Empower Your Aura.

Empowering your aura is important whenever you feel influenced by another person or the environment. Techniques to empower your aura are: place yourself in a globe of Light; see doors closing to negative people and situations; imagine your aura sparkling and bursting with Light; visualize Light flowing around you in a spiral from your feet to above your head.

From Aura Empowerment

9. Protect People or Property with Light.

If you are worried about someone's safety, see them surrounded with Light. Circle your home with Light. Place Archangel Michael all around the person or property, in front, back, above, below, to the left and right sides. Surround your vehicle with Light and Archangel Michael's presence while driving. Do this immediately if you almost have an accident or even the thought of an accident. Intend that the Light be strong, clear, and protective.

From Divine Light

10. Soften.

Soften whenever you find yourself tightening up, pulling back, or disconnecting. Softening helps you become bigger than the situation by expanding your energy through it, and connecting you to the bigger picture of what is going on. This expanded view can show you solutions and help you step out of the limitations of the problem.

From the Softening Exercise

11. Pour in Love.

Whenever you are disturbed, upset, or concerned about a person, relationship, condition, or world event, fill it with Divine Love. Say or think, "Divine Love is pouring into _____ [name the condition] now." Don't get caught in the negativity. You are not powerless. Pour Love into the situation. If you cannot do it yourself, ask Divine Mother or a favorite Divine Being to do it. This keeps you connected to Divine Energy rather than connected to the presenting negativity.

From Divine Love

12. Cut Binding Ties.

When you can't get out of recurring thoughts, emotions, or images, it helps to quickly use the Cutting Binding Ties Tool. Ask Divine Mother or Archangel Michael to cut binding ties between you and the issue. "See" or "feel" the ties being cut layer by layer until you notice relief. Cut binding ties between you and people that bother or have hurt you. Cut the ties between you and any obsessive thoughts.

From Cutting Binding Ties

13. Stop Self-Criticism.

Whenever you catch yourself thinking something like "That was a dumb thing to do … I'm hopeless … I'm an idiot," immediately stop and say good things about yourself, like "I am okay … I can handle this … am a good person … I am doing fine … know what I'm doing … I'm smart." Say the opposite of the insult you just gave yourself. Then drop it and move on.

From the Self-Love Exercise

Note: Some daily situations may aggravate deeper long-standing issues, and you will need a thorough Divine Mother Healing to dissolve them. Do this as soon as time allows to get the issue fully resolved.

Programs Offered

Welcome to the World of Divine Mother. Connie Huebner's aim is to empower you in your Divine Self. Connie offers these programs to enhance your Divine connection and help you awaken to the Divine Wisdom within.

All programs are offered online by webcast, teleconference, and Zoom, or in person in Fairfield, Iowa. To participate, go to *www.divinemotheronline.net*

Free Energy Healings - These two-hour free healings are available online and by teleconference. They provide a glimpse into the depth and power of Divine Mother's connection to you. She heals your issues while drawing you into Her heart where you are one with Her. Her Love is tangible and sweet as you let go of deep fears and other core issues in Her loving embrace. She reminds you of your Divine Nature and gives you a taste of what life with Her is like. She will shift your energy out of pain, fear, and anger, and give you knowledge of how to continue growing and changing until you reach your highest potential. Each healing is deeply purifying, and you come back into activity renewed, unburdened, and with a way to move forward with confidence and strength. The meetings end with a question-and-answer period in which Divine Mother will discuss your questions, comments, and experiences.

Feast of Light - Receive Healing and Wisdom Once a Week. Divine Mother will nourish your heart and feed your cells with Light. These one-hour sessions are a quick pick-me-up to supply you with an abundance of Divine Energy. After a thorough vibrational lift, She will provide knowledge and wisdom on a variety of timely themes. Topics include physical health, relationships, manifestation of desires, environmental and social issues, spiritual evolution, and global transformation.

Self-Healing Course - Learn to Clear Your Energy with Divine Mother's Tools. This course introduces you to Divine Mother's Healing Tools and refines your ability to use them with skill. Every Tool has special power which can be enhanced with more understanding and practice. You will learn how to use the Healing Tools for a variety of needs, for example: ancestral healing, addictions, clearing your family, your home, your pet, your office, and many other applications. This course is taught online by webcast, teleconference, and Zoom in four two-hour sessions.

Dialogue with Divine Mother Course - Every human being can learn to talk to Divine Mother. It is easy and natural to do this. In this course, you will learn how to receive Wisdom from Divine Mother by using Her Energy Tools to clear blocks to communication. You will also learn how to test the authenticity of the messages you receive. By practicing during the class, you will get used to receiving Divine Wisdom until it becomes a natural part of your life. This class aligns you with Divine Mother so that you can easily dissolve negative energy and connect to Divine Mother for guidance and support at any time.

Living in Divine Grace Course - This course takes the *Dialogue with Divine Mother Course* to the next level. You have learned how to heal yourself, as well as how to connect to Divine Mother and receive wisdom and personal guidance. *Living in Divine Grace* further develops these skills. Many students take this course to become a certified practitioner of Divine Mother Healing. Others take this course to deepen their own experience and advance their skill in healing family, friends, and the world.

In this advanced course, you learn to heal others by working directly with Divine Mother. Assisted by Connie, She personally teaches you Her Divine skills for transformation and healing. Throughout the course, students facilitate healing sessions for each other, discuss the results, and refine their ability to receive Divine Wisdom. They also learn how the Tools may be used for social, political, and environmental issues.

Prerequisite: *Dialogue with Divine Mother Course*

Ordination Course - As an Ordained Minister and Founder of Divine Mother Church, Connie offers an Ordination Program. Ordination allows you to represent Divine Mother in spiritual rituals and celebrations. As an ordinated minister in the Divine Mother Church, you are able to offer Divine Mother's Presence to all participants in any gathering.

Your spiritual experience and knowledge have been developed in the *Dialogue with Divine Mother* and *Living in Divine Grace Courses*. The **Ordination Course** trains you in how to apply this knowledge and these skills to honor the Divine in significant life passages, seasonal celebrations, and holidays. You learn the specific spiritual emphasis for all rituals and holidays to bring Divine Energies into each element of the service. Conducting every service is a beautiful experience because Divine Mother guides you, and the events you lead always vibrate with Her Love.

Prerequisite: *Living in Divine Grace Course*

Divine Mother's Ascension Program - Ascension is the full experience of your Oneness with God on all levels, physical as well as spiritual, mental, and vibrational. The physical body is maintained, but it becomes completely spiritualized. This marks the pinnacle of the evolution of your material existence. Your physical body is transmuted by filling it with Divine Energies. Ascension is a transformation at the cellular, atomic, and subatomic levels of your system.

During this program, Light is infused into your cells daily by Divine Mother, facilitated by Connie Huebner. There are weekly knowledge meetings by teleconference to provide more direct contact with Connie and Divine Mother. At these meetings, Divine Mother gives information on Ascension and your progress. She suggests "homework" to help accelerate your spiritual growth by changing the way you approach life in your thinking and behavior. She encourages you to email your experiences with the homework, and She will comment on each personal report. If you can't attend the meetings, a recording and written transcript will be emailed to you.

Ascension is the direction we are all headed. In this powerful interactive program, you will learn about the Ascension process and participate in it directly.

Many members enroll their families and friends without their knowing about it, so that they may receive the blessings of Divine Mother's focused attention every day.

Great Awakenings - Divine Mother and Connie formed this course as a graduate research group to take advanced students farther and deeper into Divine Union. Life in unity with the Divine is elegant and full of joy and wisdom. *Living in Divine Grace Course* graduates have the skills to explore deep levels of healing and to access profound Knowledge. In *Great Awakenings*, students have the opportunity to refine subtle perceptions; develop greater heart expansion; learn how to move through different dimensions; practice surrender of the small self; learn to communicate with the environment; heal local, national, and global issues; and facilitate world healings. Divine Mother is eagerly waiting to teach us about everything we can imagine and more.

Prerequisite: *Living in Divine Grace Course*

More ... Divine Mother is constantly upgrading and opening new opportunities to gain knowledge, wisdom, and deeper, more expansive use of Her Healing Tools.

Join our mailing list and stay updated on all of these programs that involve the cutting edge of consciousness and vibrational healing. To join, go to *https://divinemotheronline.net/email-updates/*

Watch Connie Huebner on Buddha at the Gas Pump at:
https://batgap.com/?s=Connie+Huebner&submit=Search

Enjoy our YouTube videos at: https://www.youtube.com/results?search_query=divinemotheronline and here: *https://www.youtube.com/user/DivineMotherOnline*

Index

About the Author

Connie Huebner grew up in western Michigan. She graduated from the University of North Carolina in Chapel Hill, where she received a BA in Political Science. Later, she completed a Master's Degree in Research in Consciousness from Maharishi European Research University in Seelisburg, Switzerland.

Connie worked full-time as a teacher of the Transcendental Meditation Program for 20 years. During that time, she joined the Unity Church and became a lay minister. She went on to become an ordained minister in the Church of the Holy Spirit and founded Divine Mother Church, a church that honors the Divine Mother in all spiritual traditions.

In her spiritual research, Connie learned to communicate with Divine Mother. In concert with Divine Mother, Connie created an energy healing program called Divine Mother Healing, a system of healing that empowers people to heal themselves and others. She now offers classes, courses, and private sessions to connect people to Divine Mother.

Connie is married with two adult children. She and her husband live in Fairfield, Iowa, where she offers the Divine Mother Guidance and Healing Programs to a world-wide audience through the Internet and her publications. Contact her through her website: *www.DivineMotherOnline.net.*